MW00378922

bush
PUBLISHING
& associates

ALL LIFE
MATTERS

My personal story of abortion,
adoption and choosing life.

DIXIE L. BRUSH

bush
PUBLISHING
& associates

ALL LIFE MATTERS

ISBN (paperback) 978-1-63752-048-2
ISBN (ebook) 978-1-64945-906-0
Copyright © 2021 by Dixie L. Brush

First printing 2021 by Bush Publishing and Associates, LLC., Tulsa, Oklahoma
www.bushpublishing.com

Bush Publishing & Associates, LLC., books may be ordered through bushpublishing.com, online and retail bookstores everywhere and on Amazon.com.

Cover Art, Layout and Design by Bush Publishing and Associates, LLC, Tulsa, Oklahoma

Editing by Writing By Michele, LLC, Tulsa, Oklahoma www.writingbymichele.com

All opinions expressed in this book are the author's.

Printed in the United States of America.

If you've ever felt hopeless, facing a situation that seems so bad, it looks like there is no way out…

If you've come to a place where there are no family and no friends who understand what you're going through…

If it feels like there is no help and you're all alone…

If you've come to the fork in the road, and it's time to CHOOSE…

Then this book is dedicated to you.

Author's Note

This is my life story. It is a true story, one which I hope will help other young girls and women to choose life instead of abortion. I was looking for love in all the wrong places, but God has loved me, consistently and deeply, throughout my lifetime. My story is certainly a testimonial to the power of prayer and God's love for us, no matter how much we have missed the mark. I pray that it encourages you, inspires you, offers you hope and leads you closer to the Lord who loves you so very, very much.

Dixie L. Brush

CONTENTS

Foreword

Of all the stories I've ever heard told, watched in a theater or read in a book, the best ones were always true. Those true stories that move you and inspire you and give you hope are about things that really happened and somehow, some way, you relate to it. They just seem to touch your heart and you shed a tear of sadness, some tears of joy, and when it's all over, you feel good inside and glad you're alive.

This is one of those stories. It all starts with a beautiful nineteen-year-old girl who falls in love with a handsome seventeen-year-old boy back in 1958. The setting is New Wilmington, Pennsylvania, which is the definition of small-town USA. There are Amish horses and buggies going down the streets, one general store, one movie house, and everyone knows everyone else's business.

The only big thing happening is that the town is home to a picturesque, down to earth, small college which makes everyone proud. One of the school's most prominent professors happens to be the father of a beautiful young lady named Dixie. In high school, she is a cheerleader and majorette, plays basketball and softball, and is the school's sweater queen. She is one of the nicest young girls on campus.

One might think that a girl as pretty and as popular as Dixie would fall in love with the handsome captain of the football team, get married, and live happily ever after. However, the truth is she fell in love with Ernie, a young teenager just out of high school.

Ernie was poor, lived at home alone with his mother, and never knew his real father. He certainly wasn't someone that Dixie's family would want her to fall in love with—but real life is stranger, and more beautiful, than fiction, and wondrous love can bloom anywhere.

The unlikely romance developed, and in October 1958, Dixie and Ernie conceived a child. Today, getting pregnant before you're married is commonplace, and no one thinks twice about it. But back in 1958, in small-town USA where everyone knows your business, especially if you're the daughter of a prominent professor at the most highly thought of college in town...

I think you get the picture.

Today, the solution would be a quick abortion and no one's the wiser. But back in 1958, the young lovers faced a definite problem with no easy solution. Because they were truly in love, Ernie and Dixie decided to get married. Together, hand in hand, they shared their situation and solution with Dixie's parents. The prominent professor and high-society wife reacted by kicking Ernie out and locking Dixie in. She was forbidden to see him, but like all true lovers they were determined to find a way somehow. Sneaking behind her parents' back, Dixie and Ernie drove out of state to get a marriage license but because of their ages, they ran into some delays, and were forced to return home.

This time, Dixie's family gave her an ultimatum that she couldn't refuse. She would go into a home for unwed mothers and give up her child. The rest of the family would move to California before the town's shame fell on them. Dixie could join them, once the baby was given up for adoption. That was the plan, and that was exactly what they did, leaving Dixie alone to deal with her pregnancy.

No one in the town knew where the family went, including Ernie. In July 1959, Dixie gave birth to an 8-pound, 10-ounce, bouncing baby boy. With no family or friends by her side, no prospects for making a living, no way to reach Ernie again, and no hope in her heart, a broken-hearted Dixie reluctantly gave up her son.

The child was adopted by a young banker and his wife, who were not able to have children of their own. He grew up only ten miles away from the same town his real mother had lived in. He even attended the same picturesque small college and played football for the same team his mother was a cheerleader for some eighteen years earlier.

This book will take you through this child's life as well as Dixie's. You'll go through the good times and the bad with them, but I can personally assure you that in the end, you'll cry tears of joy and feel good inside. You'll be glad you're alive. You'll sense you have a purpose of your own. And you will see God's hand at work in all of it, to bring about good, just as He has promised to do for us when we believe in Him.

You see, my name is Scott and I'm the bouncing baby boy in this story. Six days after my twenty-seventh birthday, I met my Mom, Dixie, for the first time since my birth. Now, we share a love and a bond that only a mother and son can share. I also met my birth father, Ernie, two weeks later. I developed a loving, warm relationship with both of them.

We have a powerful story we want to share with everyone. A miracle story with all the emotion and drama that only real life can give.

A reminder that to God, all life matters—and we all have a powerful purpose He wants for each of us to live out, for His glory and for our blessing.

May this book inspire you to protect life in every way you can.

Enjoy our story,

Scott Russell

CHAPTER ONE

Finding Scott

It's afternoon, and the mall in New Castle, Pennsylvania, is just busy enough to make me feel nervous. I slowly park my rental car, walk inside, and wander about, thinking about the person I am about to meet for the very first time in twenty-seven long years.

My firstborn son. The one I was forced to give up when I was just twenty-one and had no prospects and no way to raise him on my own.

If I stop to think about all the heartache I've faced over the years after giving him up...the sense of loss...the sorrow... the desperate prayers in the middle of the night when I couldn't sleep... If I ponder it too much, I'll probably break into tears. So I turn my thoughts instead to what my son will look like. Will he have his father's tanned skin? His curly hair? Will he have my smile? My eyes?

As I walk through the mall, I look at anyone who could be his age, wondering if this might be him. I pass stores where people shop, oblivious to what I'm going through. There are young families with their children—enjoying a life I missed with my son, but one he was able to have with a different set of parents, all because I chose not to end his life before it began. I listen to children laugh as they play and point to toys in the windows that they want.

I wonder what my son's laugh will be like. I hope I get to hear it today. I wonder if he'll be too nervous to laugh.

As I approach a bank of phones, I see a young man, tall, tanned, attractive. He has a young boy on his shoulders, and he is pacing. He seems nervous. He's staring at an elderly woman seated on a nearby bench, her straggling hair unkempt, her clothes looking ragged. A bag full of clothes, which seems like it contains all she owns, is resting beside her. The man seems to swallow hard as he prepares to approach this old woman.

This has to be my son. It has to be. Who else would approach a bag lady, looking like he's ready to hug her?

His back is to me. He hasn't seen me. I come closer, feeling butterflies in my stomach, excited and hopeful and anxious all at the same time. There's no going back. It's now or never.

So, I reach out and place my hand gently on his shoulder. And he turns to look into my eyes...

CHAPTER TWO

A Lonely Childhood

Whenever I see a young woman who is contemplating giving up her child or having an abortion, my heart goes out to her, because I know exactly what it is like to be in that woman's shoes. Many people think the woman is heartless, or just doesn't care, but I know the truth.

She's alone.

She's probably feeling so alone, her heart could break. If only she felt surrounded by love, supported by people who care about her and her unborn child. It could make all the difference!

I know this, because I lived it. I was alone when I gave up Scott so many years ago. But then, I was alone—and lonely—for so much of my life that it became a normal part of my existence. I longed to escape that feeling and find love, real love, but didn't know how. Those feelings of being lonely, rejected, and abandoned start young—very young.

For me, it began almost from the day I was born.

It was a Sunday evening in March 1938, in Ohio. My father, Donald Leo Barbe, was 32 years old, a schoolteacher. My mother, Nellie Grace Price, was 28 and a housewife. They had a five-year-old boy named Donald William and a seven-year-old girl named Donna Jean. Back then, a new house cost around $4,000. Gasoline was just ten cents a gallon. Minimum wage was only twenty-five cents an hour.

But the cost of living was still high compared to people's wages, and it was not cheap to raise children, then or now. So, my parents were entirely content to have just one son and one daughter. They certainly were not planning on having a third child. In fact, I was told in later years that I was a mistake—but I'll get to that soon enough.

Mistake or not, I came into the world that evening in March 1938, and my parents had no choice but to raise me. Mom and Dad were so unenthusiastic about having a third young mouth to feed that they hadn't even planned what to name me. Eventually, they settled on Dixie, after Bing Crosby's wife, Dixie Lee Crosby. Apparently, the news came on the radio saying she had passed away, and Mom loved Bing Crosby. So that's how I got the name Dixie Lee.

To understand how I came to give up my firstborn son, Scott, it helps to understand my early life and my family—because the pressures people experience from those around them can dramatically impact the choices they are faced with. And those pressures play a large part in why a young woman might give up a child or feel that her only option is an abortion.

My paternal grandfather's family came over from Germany in the early 1700s. They settled in Bristolville, Ohio and were dairy farmers. My grandfather's name was Don William Barbe and my grandmother's name was Nellie Grace Parker, both born in Ohio. My father, Donald Leo, was born in Ohio on June 10, 1905 and was their only child.

Life on the farm wasn't easy, and it didn't suit my father. He had to get up early and milk the cows by hand before he could walk three miles to school. He hated being a farmer, so he went to Hiram College to become a teacher. He excelled in basketball and baseball, and was even inducted into Hall of Fame at Hiram College—something he took great pride in.

My relationship with my father's side of the family was often strained. I still remember, all these years later, the day mom and dad went on vacation, and my brother, sister and I stayed with our grandparents on the farm. There was a hole in the ceiling, and in the evening, we watched the snow float through it to land on us. Being so young, I had to go to the bathroom often, but they had to take me outside to the outhouse. Needless to say, I didn't like staying overnight with them.

Whenever we visited, we always sat in a room with a potbelly wood stove in the middle of the room. My grandfather had a spittoon by his side as he lounged with his feet up on the stove. The adults would talk, and all I could do was sit and watch him spit. On one visit, I got bored. After a few hours of waiting as patiently as a toddler possibly could, I decided to ask a question.

"When are we going home?"

No one seemed to hear me. They certainly didn't respond to me. Instead, they kept chatting with each other, as though I wasn't even there. I began repeating my question, asking when we were going home, over and over. All of a sudden, my dad turned, angry, and smacked me in the face.

"Be quiet while the adults talk!" he demanded. I held my cheek, stunned. He pointed to a place in the corner where I should sit down and wait in silence. Quietly, I obeyed.

I learned from that day never to say a word while I was at my grandparents, and just sit still and let others have their way. It was a lesson I carried into the rest of my family life.

In 1923, my father married my mom, Nellie Grace Price, the daughter of Raymond Price and Icey J. Kelly. My mother was their only child. My grandfather worked on the railroad, and my grandmother was a school teacher in a small one room school. She was also a seamstress, and she sewed all my cheerleader uniforms as I grew up.

Gammy and Gampy, as I called them, practically raised me while mom and dad worked. And they were one of the few sources of love I felt I had in those early, lonely years of my childhood. Gampy enjoyed taking me with him when he went places, and he would treat me to candy. Gammy taught me how to do things, like sewing and baking.

I only remember a few stories from my early childhood—but one of them is that my maternal grandmother saved my life! When I was only about a year old, I had a terrible case of pneumonia. In those days, pneumonia could be the death knell of a child so young. It was the leading infectious cause of death in the 1930s and early 1940s. And though some treatments were beginning to come to light, it would have been unlikely to see the new drug therapies given to a child my age. Many parents, perhaps including my own, would take a wait and see attitude, not holding out much hope for their child's recovery.

But thank the Lord, my Gammy didn't give up on me. A determined woman in her own way, Gammy set about trying to cure me. Lovingly, she made a tent over my head with a bedsheet. Then she fried onions to make an old-fashioned poultice that she set gently on my chest, and stayed with me all night long to make sure I was breathing in the fumes.

Miraculously, this old-fashioned home remedy speeded up the process of clearing my lungs. The doctor couldn't believe I made it through the night, let alone that I was so much improved by the next day. If not for Gammy's nursing me, I might not be here today. And neither would my son, Scott.

Those precious moments when I knew someone cared about me came few and far between. As I grew up, I had a pervasive sense that I just wasn't welcome in my family. Even as a toddler, I seemed to have a desire to escape the restrictive rules and expectations of my parents and find my own way. I seemed always to be on my own, as one of my strongest early memories can show you.

When I was around three years old, my family went to the county fair in Canfield, Ohio. Going to the fair was the highlight of everyone's summer. It was a festive time to celebrate all the hard work of farming our neighbors did, enjoy tasty treats and see the animals. So many people gathered in large crowds to be a part of it. There were rides for the children to play on, and brand-new tractors for the adults to admire.

Shouts and laughter filled the air, and you could smell fresh, sweet cotton candy as you walked around.

That day, as we entered the fair, I walked alongside my sister Donna. My parents had instructed her to watch me and hold my hand while we were there, and she was dutifully trying to obey, though I'm sure she wasn't too excited about it. Imagine being ten years old and having to watch a three-year-old.

I didn't make it any easier on her either. I wanted to see what was happening all around me, take it all in and have fun, but I couldn't. Since I was so small and stuck walking behind a crowd of people who were taller than me, all I could see was people's legs and feet. I was missing out on seeing the cows and horses, the tractors and rides and games. Other adults might have put their sons and daughters on their shoulders to give their children a rich and colorful experience of the fair, but not my parents. No one seemed interested in letting me enjoy what was happening all around me.

Frustrated, I kept pulling my hand toward my body, hoping Donna would let go. Finally, she released me. Free of her, I looked at the crowd gathered tightly in front of me. Then I looked down a nearby alley, which was empty and easy to get to. Beyond it, I could see a clear field with lots of dirt. Without a thought, I immediately took off down the alley. When I reached the field, I looked around and saw no one else was around. It was just me. I could hear the fair in the distance, but there were no annoying crowds blocking me. What a relief!

Determined to find my own fun, I went exploring. I walked to the center of the open area, where the dirt was loose. Perfect! I knelt down and started to dig, playing a little game with myself.

Just as I started to have real fun, a man and woman came up to me and asked if I knew where my mom and dad were. I didn't recognize them, but I assumed they knew my parents, so I pointed toward the crowds and said, "Yes, they're up there somewhere." They looked at me funnily, but they continued on their way, and I continued to play.

Then, out of nowhere, another man showed up. "Come here, little girl," he said. Before I could protest, he picked me up and carried me to a small stand where announcements could be made to the crowds of people. "Now, what's your name?" he asked.

I didn't say a word.

"Sweetheart, what's your name? Where are your mommy and daddy?"

I wanted to run away but he wouldn't release me, and I started to cry.

"Oh, no, dear, don't do that!" The man tried tickling me as he asked my name again, probably thinking I'd find that comforting, but I didn't. I got so upset and cried even harder. Frustrated, the man picked up a bullhorn and began talking into it. All the while, I continued to weep and wail.

All of a sudden, I saw my dad running across the field as he came to get me. I was so relieved, mainly because the man on the podium finally stopped tickling me and let me go.

Later, I found out the fair's gates were closed by the police at my grandfather's request until they found me. They said that the pretty field I was digging in was the racetrack and the horses were about to come out when they found me playing in the dirt. My poor sister got into trouble for not holding my hand. My parents were angry with me, of course, and embarrassed by all the commotion I had caused.

I couldn't understand what any of the fuss was about. In my mind, I had simply been having fun.

Since my sister and brother were so much older than me, I found myself playing alone most of the time. I felt like an only child because no one, especially my sister and brother, never wanted me around them. My parents were always so busy working—Mom was a hairdresser, and Dad worked at a wax paper company until he became a teacher—that they could barely keep up with Donna and Bill's school activities.

As a result, I didn't get a lot of time with any of them. Instead, I was often sent to stay with my grandmother and grandfather for the day. To be honest, I really enjoyed going there because they paid so much attention to me. My grandparents taught me about animals, bugs, and all the other mischievous things an adventurous little girl like me wanted to know about.

When I went back home, though, no one seemed to notice I was even there. Donna and Bill never wanted to play with me. In fact, I sometimes felt that my siblings disliked me. Even my parents weren't particularly attached to me. One day, I realized it was because they hadn't wanted a third child. My brother and I had been talking with my mother about the age difference between us—there was just two years' difference between Donna and Bill, but five years between him and me.

"Why did you wait so long to have her?" Bill asked, impudent as ever.

My mother admitted the truth. "We didn't plan on having Dixie. She was an accident."

She went on to explain further, not that it made me feel any better. My father had only wanted one child, so when Donna was born, he was satisfied. But Mom wanted a boy, so she tricked Dad and became pregnant with Bill. Dad wasn't exactly happy to have a second child, but he could at least appreciate having a boy as well as a girl, so he accepted Bill after a while.

But neither of them wanted a third child. They hadn't planned on having me, and they weren't happy when Mom unexpectedly became pregnant a third time. The Great Depression had made things difficult on them, and they couldn't afford another child, so when I came along, it created an unbearable strain on them.

I was an accident. A mistake. And my parents resented me for it. I suppose that their resentment became absorbed by my brother and sister too. No wonder I felt so rejected.

With Bill, what I faced was often even worse than just rejection. He could be violent and even dangerous.

I first became afraid of him when I was around five years old. At that age, I was already stubborn. When I wouldn't do what Bill wanted, he would find a way to scare me until I gave in to him.

One day, Bill and I were in the garage. We certainly weren't playing; Bill was hitting me with a yardstick in an effort to get me to say "uncle." It hurt, and I didn't like it. But I wasn't going to give in and say uncle. When I refused, Bill became furious with me. Suddenly, he threw down the yardstick, pushed me down on the floor and put a pillow over my face.

I couldn't breathe—and I was terrified! Realizing I couldn't help myself or get away, I finally just lay there and stopped fighting him. After what seemed like an hour of fear and agony, he finally let me up. Someone had come looking for us since we'd been gone so long. I jumped up and ran away, crying. I had always thought Bill hated me, but now I was sure of it.

Sadly, my parents never knew how my brother treated me as a kid. They were never there to observe it, but I sometimes wonder if they would have done anything to stop it, even if they had known.

In 1944, I started first grade in Minerva, Ohio. My maternal grandfather always walked me to the swinging bridge that went over the creek near the school and sent me on my way. The older kids would make the bridge swing as they walked across, and it would scare me to death.

The first day of school, as I went across the bridge with my new pencil box in hand, the older kids started making the bridge swing. I fell down onto my hands and knees, crying in fear. My new pencil box fell into the creek, lost for good. Finally, one of the girls made the boys stop swinging the bridge so I could continue on my way to school. To this day, I'm still afraid of swinging bridges.

Only a few months after I began first grade, my family moved to New Wilmington, Pennsylvania, a small college town where my dad was hired as a professor of speech and dramatics at Westminster College. I was just six years old.

New Wilmington was a quaint small town. The college, its main attraction, had a lovely campus with beautiful, elegant stone buildings. There were no street lights. Cars had to maneuver around Amish horse-and-buggies from the Amish settlement nearby. There was a town swimming pool, one movie theater which was open on Saturdays for Western matinees, one grocery store, one hangout for college students and high school kids called the Grill, and one restaurant called the Tavern. A few hundred people in all lived there—and everyone knew everyone else, a trait that can be both good and bad.

Mom and Dad bought an old two-story house with three bedrooms and one bath overlooking the park and swimming pool. My grandmother and grandfather bought a house across the street from us, so we were together again. Yet I still felt alone.

I finished first grade in New Wilmington. It was a lonely mile to school, yet I walked it by myself every single day, even in rain and snow. My sister and brother were supposed to walk with me, but they would always go ahead of me because I walked too slowly for them. As usual, I was left behind to fend for myself.

One winter day that year, I had no gloves or boots to wear, but I still carried my books in my freezing hands the long mile to school. When I got to class, I was crying because I was so cold. My teacher tried to warm me up and soothed me so I would stop crying. She must have reported the situation to my parents because after that, I always had gloves and boots.

In contrast to my difficulties at home, I loved school and my classmates. It was one of the first times I felt a sense of connection and belonging. I was part of a group of three girls and three boys who did everything together from first grade to twelfth grade. We played kick the can, hide and seek, and softball. We swam. We blocked off a road so we could go sledding during the winter, and went to Saturday afternoon western matinees. It was a wonderful break from my unhappy home.

Still, in the midst of all my childhood heartbreaks, there was one thing that stood out as redeeming—my discovery of God.

I first heard about Sunday school and God from Jerry, one of the boys in my second-grade class. Our fathers taught together at Westminster College, and they were friends. My parents and his parents would play cards every Saturday night, and Jerry would come over to play with me. He and I became friends, and so it was not too surprising when Jerry asked me to go to Sunday School with him the next day— and I got to go!

It was my first experience of getting to know God. I listened closely in Sunday School and enjoyed my time there. After that first time in church, I wanted to go back. Something about it made me feel a connection to things bigger than me. Of course, I didn't understand it at the time. It was only later in life that I came to appreciate what it meant to have faith in God. As a child, I simply knew I felt something powerful when I went to church, and I wanted to experience it more.

I also wanted to understand God better. It wasn't easy, because many of the ideas taught in church were too complicated for a child to grasp. I didn't know how God could be in Heaven and be our Father too. I didn't know what the Sunday School teacher meant when she said that Jesus died for our sins so that we would have eternal life in Heaven. These were new ideas to me, and not always easy to understand.

But God has a way of revealing Himself to us that makes Him easy to relate to—and child-like faith can open that door to having a close relationship with Him. As a child, I discovered this firsthand, and it's a pretty miraculous story that I love sharing with others to show how much God cares about even the littlest things that matter to you and me.

I can remember to this day the first time I prayed to God. On one hot summer Saturday, I was swinging outside in the hammock while everyone else was inside cleaning the house. My brother Bill had a parakeet named Blue Boy, and he had hung the cage outside to give the bird some air and make space while he cleaned inside.

I sat there watching the bird for the longest time. Blue Boy kept throwing his little body against the cage door, like he wanted to get out. I felt sorry for the bird—perhaps I could relate to how trapped he felt. So I opened the door and watched in awe as he flew out and landed on a limb high in the tree. Too high for me to reach and get him back.

At first, I thought Blue Boy would fly back into the cage when he got tired, but I was wrong. After a while, I finally realized he wouldn't get back in the cage when I called his name—and then he flew away! I looked for him but couldn't find him anywhere. He was gone.

"Oh no!" I moaned. "Oh no!" Knowing I would be in terrible trouble with my mother and my brother when they found out, I began to cry harder than I had ever cried before.

All of a sudden, I heard a little voice say to me, "Ask God."

To this day, I'm not sure exactly how I would have thought to ask God to help me. All I can imagine is that the teacher in Sunday School must have explained to us that God answers prayers. Somehow, though, in His infinite faithfulness and love for little children, He was reaching out to encourage me.

I stopped crying then, just long enough to ask Him to bring Blue Boy back and help me get him back in the cage. I promised I would never let the little parakeet out again. Then I cried myself to sleep on the hammock, still mouthing that desperate prayer to a God I barely knew.

A while later, I awoke to the sound of a bird tweeting and chirping, like he couldn't be any happier. Slowly, I opened my eyes and looked around. And there was Blue Boy, hanging on the side of the cage. I didn't want to startle him into flying away, so instead of jumping out of the hammock, I moved very carefully. Slowly, I approached him and gently opened the cage door and stepped back. I watched in amazement and relief as he hopped right inside and started drinking water. I didn't realize it at the time, but God answered my prayer. Ask, and you shall receive!

Shortly after that miracle with Blue Boy, which I never shared with anyone, we began going to church more often. Mom went with me, for she didn't want me to walk the mile to church alone. But rather than allowing me to go to a Sunday School class, she insisted I had to sit beside her in the adult service. I didn't understand what was going on in those services, and I got really bored. But God still continued to show Himself to me in ways that a child could understand.

One Sunday, I listened to the minister as he explained how God watches over his ministers as they are preaching. As I watched him preaching in the pulpit, I saw a shadowy figure standing behind him, one hand resting on his shoulder. I was shocked—especially when I looked around and realized the adults were acting completely calm about it. They couldn't see what I was seeing!

I leaned over to tell Mom about what I saw, but I stopped myself from doing so for two reasons. One was simple in the eyes of a child: I wasn't allowed to talk in church. She'd get angry. The other reason was more heart-breaking: I knew she wouldn't believe me. So I kept what I had seen to myself and pondered on it for a long time, like Mary must have pondered on what the angel Gabriel told her.

After that special experience, I wanted to understand God more than ever. But at around this time, Mom suddenly stopped going to church. At first, I didn't understand why. Eventually, I came to realize it was because the minister kept coming to the house and asking her to send in her tithe. She didn't have the money he was asking for, so she simply stopped going to church.

For a while, I continued going alone. But I had to walk that lonely mile by myself, and in winter it was simply too hard for a second-grader like me to manage. I remember slipping in the ice and snow, falling, and hurting myself. It was frightening! Reluctantly, I made the decision not to walk to church again. My parents were just fine with that, preferring to sleep in on Sundays anyway. For a long time after that, I didn't attend church or feel connected to God, though I longed to do so.

In 1950, I was old enough to notice that the town of New Wilmington was divided into two groups. There was the upper-class college group, made up of teachers like my father and my family. Those of us who belonged to this group lived in an area of town that everyone else in town sarcastically referred to as Snob Hill. The rest of the town was on the outside looking in. Those who were not as educated, or didn't have a white-collar job, or were somehow or other considered lower class in status were looked down upon by my parents and their friends.

I didn't care about these differences. But it was almost impossible to ignore them, because everyone else in town cared so much about them. My parents cared deeply about it, that was certain. They knew we lived on Snob Hill, and they wanted to do whatever they could to stay there.

My father was promoted to head of the speech and dramatics department at Westminster College, a prestigious achievement that he was very proud of. Mom began working in the college's administration department. They remained very busy with Donna and Bill's activities, even at the college level. Everything revolved around what was happening at Westminster. Mom served as a sorority mother for my sister's sorority, handling all their activities. Bill was an actor in all of the plays that Dad was directing and producing. As usual, they all barely had time for me, and I was left to fend for myself however I could.

Around fifth grade, the friends I spent time with began to pair off. One of the boys, Bob Brush, and I spent all of our time together, in school and out. We often went to the movies together, and we would hold hands as he walked me the mile home. I enjoyed his company so much. But I wouldn't allow him to walk me to my home's front door because I was afraid of what my mother would do or say if she found out how close we were. She didn't approve of him as a boyfriend because he and his family weren't members of the upper class and they weren't connected with Westminster College. Even as a child, it seemed as if I would find people to connect with, only to see them slip away.

When I was in eighth grade, a new boy named Bob V. moved into town, and things suddenly changed for me. Bob V.'s father took on the position of dean at Westminster College, so naturally my parents made friends quickly with him and his wife. Bob V. was a sophomore in high school and played on the basketball team. I was a cheerleader, so we got to know each other. I was allowed to date him because his family belonged to the upper class, college society my parents cared so much about fitting into.

Bob V. and I began dating, and for five years, we went everywhere together. He was my first true puppy love. Bob was very religious, so we attended church together every Sunday. I got baptized, joined the Presbyterian church and joined a young people's group. We sang in the choir and helped with the younger children. This precious time with him and God meant so much to me. I felt so loved and appreciated. Bob V. gave me the attention and love I had been looking for all my life, but had never received from my family.

Sadly, though, this newfound sense of belonging didn't last. Bob's family moved to Holland, Michigan—and suddenly, my world started to fall apart. Bob convinced his parents to let him stay in New Wilmington to complete his senior year in high school. After that, he would attend college in Michigan. Bob and I were inseparable that year. In fact, we were planning on completing our education and getting married.

But things changed after he graduated and moved away. Trying to stay together when we were so far apart was hard. We wrote letters back and forth, of course, communicating as much as we could but in the end, it just wasn't enough. The distance got to us both. Finally, during my senior year of high school we broke up because we were going in different directions. We parted as friends and went our separate ways.

After we broke up, I was lost and heartbroken. We had done so much together, and now I was alone again. I felt I had lost the one person I could rely on, the one person who loved me. It was such a struggle. I was so lonely. And I didn't know if I would ever find someone else who loved me.

To try to stem my loneliness and sadness, I buried myself in high school activities and worked at the Tavern in town as a waitress for seventy-five cents an hour. Back then, that was a pretty decent salary for a teenager. I was a cheerleader too, a majorette, and a member of the softball, volleyball and basketball teams. I had roles in my junior and senior play productions as well, something I would have expected my father to be interested in, since he taught drama classes. Yet my family never came to any of my activities because they were always too busy at the college and with their own lives to pay any attention to what was happening in mine.

My response to this as a child was to try to please my family and siblings. I was definitely a people-pleaser. I remember my grandfather would pay my brother to mow his yard. When I mowed our yard, I would notice my grandfather was upset because his yard wasn't done. So I went over and mowed my grandfather's lawn to please him, but my brother got paid. I would clean the house, help take care of both yards, run errands—everything I could do to please my family and have them notice that I was in this family also. I just wanted them to care.

But with my family, this seemed to do no good. On one rare occasion, I tried to stand up for myself, and I still remember it like it was just yesterday. My family was having Sunday dinner, and everyone was talking about what they were doing at the college—Dad's plays, Mom's job, Donna's sorority, Bill's activities. None of them even bothered to look in my direction, much less ask me how my classes and work were going.

Something inside me snapped. I slammed my fork down, stood up and declared, "Why don't you ask me how I'm doing? I'm in this family too, you know. You never ask me how my day went, or what I'm doing, or how I feel."

They simply stared at me, stunned by my sudden outburst. I was usually so quiet that I don't think they even knew how to respond to what I'd said. It was so rare that I fought for myself that way. But it didn't change anything.

In fact, the only time I can remember seeing any of my family coming to one of my activities was when I was in the running for sweater queen during my junior year of high school. Back then, our school's sweater queen was like the homecoming queen is today. Each class would vote for three girls they wanted to represent them in the sweater queen's court. The queen was selected from the junior class, and the four senior high classes voted for the queen and who would be in her court. I borrowed a black sweater from my sister for the competition.

I was waiting to march on stage to participate in the ceremony when I looked toward the door and saw my mother and sister standing there waiting to see who won. It made my day to see them there! When I heard my name announced as that year's New Wilmington Sweater Queen, I was so happy—not only because I won, but more importantly, because someone from my family came to see me and share in my special moment of success.

Still, those moments of happiness came few and far between. I still felt so alone. When I was lonely and confused, I had a favorite place to go to meditate and talk to God and the Holy Spirit in the way I knew how. New Wilmington had a beautiful, serene small creek that ran from the park and town swimming pool, under the main road and bridge, past the Westminster College tennis courts, and clear past the football stadium. I would pass this bridge every day on my way home.

Whenever I needed some comfort, I would go under the bridge, sit against the wall and pray for guidance. Then I would watch the minnows as they swam so peacefully, without any cares in the world. After a while, I would look for rocks I thought were pretty, and then I'd head home. I always felt refreshed after these times of quiet meditation, and I realized God loved me, even if my family didn't.

CHAPTER THREE

True Love Lost

So much of my youth was consumed with the desire to simply be loved. I couldn't obtain the love, respect and caring I desperately needed from my family. And though I understood intellectually that God cared about me, I didn't understand Him or have a close relationship with Him or with a church. So I continued to try to find my own way in the world, testing others to see if I could find at least one person who would always love me and be there for me. And I did find someone that I thought might be the one.

During my years of high school and college, I worked at restaurants in town to earn spending money and pay for my college tuition. As a senior in high school, I left my job at the Tavern and went to work instead at the Grill, a cute little casual restaurant owned by a divorced woman and her mother. The Grill was where the college and high school students would hang out, and I worked there during school and summer break, filling up my time as much as I could to distract myself, since I missed Bob V. so much.

For a while, I dated my boss's son, Phil, who was a year behind me in school. I saw more of his mother and grandmother than I did my own family. But as usual, it wasn't meant to be. We broke up after my senior prom, and I lost another chance at what I thought could be love.

After my high school graduation in 1956, I continued to work during the summer at the Grill, helping Phil's grandmother, and earning more college money. That fall, I began attending Westminster College as a freshman. One of the highlights of my time there was attending the chapel services that took place every day at one p.m. Those daily reminders that there was a God watching over me were encouraging, at least temporarily.

But during my time in college, I was so very lonely. There were so many students in my class that I felt intimidated, self-conscious, and even scared to be there. I was so used to my small high school class, which had a mere fifty-four students total, and I missed seeing the friends I went to school with for twelve years. It was a challenging adjustment to make, being at a college with so many people, and none of them were close friends.

Once again, I tried to figure out how to make connections that would help me fight the great aching loneliness in my soul. I joined all the activities I could to meet new friends and keep busy. But with so many other students competing for the same activities, it was difficult to find a place that suited me and made me feel welcome.

I tried out for cheerleading, something I'd enjoyed doing in high school. Fifty other girls tried out too, and I found out that only one of us would be chosen to join the cheerleading squad. What pressure! We waited two full weeks after tryouts before the cheerleader was chosen and her name was put up on the gym bulletin board. I ran down to the gym every day, waiting and hoping to see my name. Finally, my name was officially posted on the bulletin board for all to see! I was the first freshman ever chosen for the team. It was a huge accomplishment and I was so happy—but I heard nothing from my family. No praise, nothing.

Next, I tried out for the synchronized swimming team and got selected for that as well. I also joined the Sigma Kappa Sorority, though I knew my mom and sister wouldn't like it because they belonged to Kappa Delta. Honestly, that was one of the reasons I joined the Sigma Kappa. I wanted to make them mad, and I also wanted to be someplace different from where they were so connected. Next, I joined the basketball and volleyball teams, trying to find where I belonged and where I could find the companionship I longed for.

Once again, my family never came to any of my events in college. Sadly, none of this was a surprise, but it still hurt me deeply, a wound I didn't think I'd ever recover from. I dated in college too, like the other girls I knew, but I never found the companionship I needed.

During this time, I also longed to find other places to meet new people—and one of those potential spots was at the local dances. My brother Bill was a dancer, quite professional at it actually, and now that he was older and not as violent toward me, he was easier to get along with. He taught me how to dance, and I loved feeling confident on my feet on the dance floor. New Wilmington would hold a monthly dance at one of the churches, and I desperately wanted to go so I could have some fun.

"Please take me," I begged him. "I won't bother you. I just want to go."

Bill rolled his eyes and tried to ignore me. "No, no," he'd say. "I'm not taking you."

But I was as stubborn and persistent as I'd ever been. I kept asking him, promising him to give him no trouble if he'd only agree to let me go with him. After begging and insisting over and over, I finally convinced Bill to take me to one of these events.

That day, I was so thrilled. I dressed up in a smart little dress that I felt made me look good, and I went with Bill to the dance, delighted to have a new experience and possibly meet new people. I looked around the room, admiring the colorful decorations, the streamers and flowers. And I watched the dancers sway to the music as they enjoyed each other's company. It was magnificent.

As I stood there taking it all in, I couldn't help noticing one of the boys in particular. He was such a good dancer, good looking with curly dark hair, and he was always smiling. I kept hoping he would ask me to dance, but he didn't. Needless to say, I was disappointed. I went home, deciding not to give him another thought.

The next day while I was at work, I looked up to see this young man enter through the doorway of the Grill. I was so excited to see him. He sat down and asked for a soda, his dark eyes sparkling as he gazed at me. The Grill was quiet at that moment, and empty. We were the only ones there, so I served him his soda and then sat with him and chatted. We were able to talk for a long time.

In a way, it was like a first date. I found out his name was Ernie Nelson Black. He lived with his mother in Volant, a town that was about eight miles east of New Wilmington where I lived. It turned out he had either hitched a ride or walked the eight miles to the Grill, because he didn't have a car of his own. He had just graduated high school but he didn't have a job yet. He was exactly the type of person my parents wouldn't want me dating—but I was smitten with him, and he with me.

Ernie and I dated from the summer of 1956 to 1959, and we enjoyed our time together so much. We had such fun together, and he was so attentive and kind to me. I felt like I had finally found someone who would be there for me when I needed him. On my lunch breaks that summer, we would go to Westminster College's tennis courts to play a round. As athletic as he was, he would beat me every time. He played basketball and golf, and he was very good in everything he set his hands to do.

We continued to see each other every day, even after my second year of college began. Always a gentleman, Ernie would wait for me to finish work and walk me home late at night. He attended all of my sporting events and activities, taking a great interest in everything I did. It was wonderful to be with Ernie and feel confident that someone cared and loved me.

Naturally, my family got in the way—when they finally realized what was happening, that is. It took a while because they just didn't pay much attention to my life or show any interest in me. My parents didn't even notice that I was seeing Ernie until I finally brought him home to meet them, months after we'd been spending time together.

Of course, as soon as Mom and Dad met him and realized he was from a poor family in Volant, they were against me dating him. Ernie wasn't a member of our college society. Worse, he looked Italian—and in the 1940s and 1950s, Italians were often discriminated against. To top it all off, Ernie didn't have a job or transportation. In every way, he was simply not good enough for their upper-class group.

After a tense, awkward evening, Ernie left. He politely bid my parents goodbye. As soon as he was gone, my parents furiously insisted that I break it off. "What on earth do you think you're doing? You can't keep seeing that boy," they told me.

"But he's so kind to me, and sweet, and—"

"It doesn't matter, Dixie! That boy is not good enough for you. He's not acceptable. We forbid you to date him anymore."

When my parents said such things, it was final. There was no point in continuing to argue. But I adored Ernie. So instead of doing as my parents said, I kept seeing him—I just did it behind their backs. Ernie and I continued to spend time with each other, though we remained quiet about it so we could be together.

In 1958, I completed my two-year secretarial degree, and I began hunting for a job. My instructor called me into his office and suggested that I interview for IBM, which had an office in Youngstown, Ohio—a thirty-minute drive from New Wilmington. It was a great idea. I got the job, but since it was located out of town, I had to get a car. This turned out to be a significant development, as I'll explain in a moment.

In the three years we dated, Ernie and I had grown serious about each other. We wanted to be together. However, my parents still refused to give me their permission to see him, and in those days, that mattered quite a bit. If Ernie and I were going to make things work between us, we realized that we needed to keep it a secret. We weren't going to let my family's opinions keep us apart. Unfortunately, Ernie wasn't yet twenty-one years old, which meant we couldn't get legally married in Pennsylvania without my parents' permission. But that didn't stop us. As young people often do, we were intimate with one another, even though we weren't married.

Because Ernie couldn't find a job in Pennsylvania, he enlisted in the U.S. Marines, while I continued to work at IBM. In this way, we thought we'd be able to take care of ourselves until we could get married. Then, the unthinkable happened—although I suppose we should have expected it.

I found out that I was pregnant.

After the initial shock had worn off, Ernie and I talked everything over and made a careful plan. Since he would be leaving for boot camp very soon, we had to act quickly. We decided to get married before he left to enter the Marines, so that we could eventually raise our baby together. We were in love anyway—true love, I believed—so the idea of getting married right away appealed to both of us.

Unfortunately, Ernie and I weren't yet twenty-one years old, which meant we couldn't get legally married in Pennsylvania without our parents' permission. So, we drove my car, the one I had fortunately bought to use for work, and we left for West Virginia after work on Friday, because we'd heard that in West Virginia, we didn't have to be twenty-one or have our parents' permission to get married. I told my mother I was spending the weekend with my coworker in Youngstown. Ernie's cousin and his wife came with us as witnesses.

But when we arrived at the courthouse, we faced an unpleasant surprise. We found out there was a three-day waiting period after applying for a marriage license before we could be married. And the courthouse was closed until Monday, so we couldn't even apply for the license until then. Unfortunately, I had to be back at work, and at home, on Monday. If we tried to wait the three days, my parents would know I had lied to them, and who knew what they might do if they found out I had run off with Ernie? I didn't want to create worse problems that I already had to face, so Ernie and I reluctantly returned to Pennsylvania, unmarried.

In the 1950s, unwed mothers were shunned, a disgrace to the family and the talk of the town. We knew we had to tell my folks, but I was scared. Once my pregnancy was known, the whole town would turn on my parents. It would be humiliating for them. How would they ever forgive me?

To his credit, Ernie wanted to come with me to tell my folks what had happened. Perhaps he held some small hope that my parents would relent and give us permission to be married. But I knew my mother would make a scene, so I told him no. I walked into the house, gathered my parents, and finally told them the truth that I was pregnant and that the father was Ernie, the boy they despised.

As you can imagine, all hell broke loose. Mom called me every name in the book, and I felt I deserved all her scorn.

"How could you do this? What were you thinking?" She and Dad couldn't get over what I had done. If the town found out, my parents would be humiliated. My family would be ruined. They couldn't believe I would do that to them. I tried to explain the situation as I saw it—through the eyes of my relationship with Ernie.

"But I love him! And I'm going to marry him!"

"Oh, no, you're not!"

I was forbidden to communicate with Ernie. Mom called a family meeting. My grandparents who lived across the street from us came over. My sister Donna came from where she lived with her husband, about twenty minutes away in Grove City, Pennsylvania. My brother Bill drove in from Pittsburgh, where he was working as a teacher.

Without my knowledge, my mother told my brother to bring a special medication with him. I found out later that my brother had some unsavory connections, including a doctor who performed illegal abortions. So, when the family meeting took place, my entire family had gathered against me. My mother, father, grandmother, grandfather, sister and brother-in-law, and brother all sat there judging me and finding me sadly wanting. Bill presented us all with the medication he had obtained from his doctor friend. My family discussed it and decided that everything would be ok if I just had an abortion. The town wouldn't know anything, and everyone in the family could go on with their lives as usual.

Except, of course, for me—because unlike them, I would not be ok. I didn't want an abortion. I wanted to get married. I wanted my baby!

I sat there, stunned, staring at them in disbelief. My heart was broken, so hurt, because once again they weren't thinking about me or what I wanted. The longer they talked, the angrier I got. Finally, I stood up and told them in no uncertain terms, "I am having my baby! Under no circumstances am I going to take that awful medicine you are trying to force on me."

They tried to reason with me and insist that I have the abortion. I stood there, my hand covering my belly protectively, just me against all of them.

Bill became angry because he had spent his rent money to get the medication, and now I was refusing to take it. "How could you do this after all I've done for you?" he wondered. He must have thought I was ungrateful, though I certainly had never asked him for that kind of help. If he had offered first or asked my opinion, I would have refused, and he wouldn't have been out that money.

The more he pushed me to take the medication that would cause an abortion, the more something inside of me grew more determined not to do it. "My baby was conceived out of love!" I yelled, infuriated with all of them. "This baby is a gift from God and has every right to live!"

They all stared at me in shock. I guess they didn't think I'd fight them. The meeting ended, no decisions made except one. My family now refused to talk to me.

For a time, this unpleasant stalemate continued. I refused to take the abortion concoction, and no one was happy about my decision. At one point, my grandmother took me quietly aside to talk with me in private. She revealed to me that she had once used a potion like the one Bill had brought home, to abort her own baby years earlier.

"We couldn't afford another child because of the Depression," she confided. "I know how hard this is for you. But it's the right decision. I will fix the potion up for you if you want it."

I told her no.

My family refused to talk with me after that. It was awful. But when I thought about the child growing inside of me, I simply knew what I had to do. I had made up my mind. Somehow, someway, even if everyone abandoned me, I would have this baby.

Soon, I turned twenty-one. And on the day of this momentous birthday, a strange thing happened. Donna and Bill took me out for dinner.

I was completely surprised by this. Up until that day, they had all been so upset with me, and none of the family had spoken to me since the meeting when I refused to have an abortion. Yet now, my sister and brother were doing something for me that many people would consider kind.

It didn't take long to figure out that they had ulterior motives. Over dinner in this public place where they knew I wouldn't make a scene, they made an announcement.

"We're moving," they said.

Apparently, behind my back, they had all been conferring and making a plan, and now it was set in stone. The entire family—Mom, Dad, Bill, Donna, her husband Richard, and my grandparents—all of them were leaving New Wilmington and moving across the country to California.

I sat there, speechless, as Donna and Bill told me all about it. While I had been waiting for them to allow me to marry Ernie, they had all quietly planned their move. They quit their jobs, sold their homes, packed their belongings and called a moving company. They were going, and there was nothing I could do to stop them.

Every single one of them had decided to move away from New Wilmington, without saying a word to anyone, to avoid any hint of scandal. This was the way of doing things in those times and in my family. Their high position in our small town meant that they were extremely concerned about appearances. Their way of dealing with something that was potentially difficult or embarrassing was not to say anything about it, and not to let anyone know the truth. It didn't matter if their decision broke my heart, as long as they protected their reputation.

Then, Bill and Donna revealed the final coup de grace that did me in. While my family was heading to California, I would not be allowed to go with them.

"Where am I supposed to go?" I asked.

"You'll go to the unwed mothers' home in Youngstown, Ohio," they announced. There I would live until I had my baby. While I sat there, trying to take it all in, they continued to explain just how things were going to work.

"You have two choices, Dixie," they told me. "Have the baby and give up the baby for adoption, and when you're done, you can come out to California and stay with all of us. We'll pretend it never happened, and you'll never talk about it again."

"What's the other choice?" I asked reluctantly, knowing it wouldn't be pretty.

They laughed at me. "Well, you can keep your baby if you want to. But we're not having anything to do with it. You'll have to stay here and figure out a way to support yourself, because you'll get no help from us."

I suddenly felt nauseated, and I pushed my plate away, dismayed and frightened.

You see, this choice they gave me might not seem like a difficult decision to make today. But in the 1950s, things were much harder for a single mother. I had no money of my own except what I earned from my salary. In those days, there was no paid pregnancy leave at IBM; you had to quit and lose your job. With a baby to care for, no job, no family support and no Ernie, it would be impossible to support myself and care for the child I was carrying.

Ernie had already left to attend the Marines boot camp, and he couldn't leave to come help me. Since we weren't already married, I couldn't go to him or stay on a military base with other military wives. His mother couldn't afford to help me, and it would have been too much of a burden for her. My family could afford it, but they refused to be involved. There would be no one to help care for and pay for the baby's needs, much less my own.

Broken-hearted, I decided I had to concentrate on what was best for the baby and myself. So I agreed to go to the unwed mothers' home in Youngstown and give up the child I had for adoption. There was no other choice.

CHAPTER FOUR

"Please Let Me Know He's OK"

As we pulled up to the Florence Crittenton unwed mothers' home in Youngstown, I felt like every inch of me was on edge. To be blunt about it, I was terrified. Being abandoned was one of the things I feared most in my life, and now my family was leaving me behind and fleeing the East Coast. They'd be hours away by plane should anything happen to me. And I wasn't sure they'd come, even if something did happen and I needed them.

The home looked a lot like a regular house. Though it was larger than the average home, it had windows with curtains, a porch entrance, and a grass lawn. It looked remarkably normal from the outside. My circumstances for being there, though, were anything but normal.

My mother and sister had driven me there, and they hardly said a word to me the entire trip. Once we parked in front of the home, they coldly instructed me to get out of the car. Dad, Bill, Donna and her husband, and my grandparents were all waiting for their return so they could leave New Wilmington—a caravan ready to head to California, without me. I pulled my suitcase out, nervous and sad. I barely had a chance to say goodbye before they abandoned me and vanished, leaving me alone to climb up the porch steps and step through the front door.

Inside, the home felt strange and foreign, full of unwed mothers-to-be like me. It was cold, dingy, dark and unwelcoming. I remember that all the women there were staring at me when I walked in.

The one thing that united us all was that we were pregnant. The home's residents were a mixture of all sorts of women—many the likes of whom I'd never interacted with before. Among us, our group spanned a wide range of ages—from a mere ten years old (I can't imagine how awful her situation must have been) to women in their late forties who simply couldn't keep a baby for whatever reasons. One of the ladies had been sentenced to prison, and was staying at the home only long enough to have her baby. After that, she'd go right back to jail. Another was a call girl whose pimp came and took her away as soon as she'd delivered her child, even though that was against the house rules.

Living at the home was a scary, nerve-wracking experience. The place was divided into two long hallways—one with rooms and beds for women coming into the home for the first time so they could become adjusted to everything. Since I was only four and a half months' pregnant, this is where they put me. All the beds were lined up on both sides and filled. The other hallway was for the mothers who were ready to give birth. Since I didn't fully understand what was happening and was so unhappy and frightened, I didn't sleep well for much of the time I was there.

While we waited to give birth, we were all assigned a set of chores to do each day. We had rules to follow, and time to kill waiting for our babies to arrive, so we swept, scrubbed floors, dusted, and cooked meals.

My assigned chores were to scrub the floors and halls. Apparently, I was also supposed to take care of the dining room where the staff ate. But when the staff member told me my responsibilities, she neglected to explain to me what I was supposed to do in the dining room. When I failed to do it, I got in trouble. Soon, I adjusted to the routine of it all. I felt like a prisoner, but there wasn't much I could do about it.

One of my biggest challenges was to avoid being recognized. IBM was located just up the street from the home, and people knew me there. Of course, I had quit that job right before I moved into the unwed mothers' home. As far as anyone at work knew, I was moving to California with my family. They didn't know I was pregnant, and I wasn't going to tell them.

But being so near the office was worrisome. I was afraid that if I went out of the house, even to take a walk, someone from my former life would recognize me. I was ashamed, and I was afraid my family would refuse to take me in again if I were discovered by my former coworkers. In fact, one time a repairman came to the home from IBM to work on some of the office equipment, and I recognized him. I ran and hid around the corner so he wouldn't see me. And I rarely went outside to avoid being spotted by anyone I knew.

At least I wasn't totally alone while I was there. I became friends with a very outgoing woman, who was due about the same time I was. We enjoyed chatting with one another. And she had a tough story of her own—her pregnancy was due to a rape, and she wanted nothing to do with the baby. She gave birth before I did, so she got to leave while I had to stay behind. I found out later that her family adopted the baby and only told her about it years later.

Another friend I made was a very young girl, just ten years old and pregnant. My heart went out to her because I knew she had it even tougher than I did. She and I would go in the TV room together and watch TV before going to bed.

Naturally, I never had any visitors because my family was gone, Ernie was in the Marines, and none of my friends knew what had happened to me. But the families of my friends at the unwed mothers home would come to visit them. They would include me in their activities, and I was so grateful to be included.

At times, there were also moments when life was normal and good things happened to give each of us a little glimmer of hope. I remember in particular that one of the mothers staying in the home was keeping her baby. She and her husband actually got married at the home after she gave birth, and then left with their baby. I was able to attend the ceremony.

A part of me was so happy for her. The other part felt heartbroken. If only Ernie and I could have had a happy ending like that. But it just wasn't meant to be.

My due date was July fourth, but I was almost three weeks late. Giving birth in that sterile, unwelcoming unwed mothers home was an experience I'll never forget—and it was terrifying.

I was in labor all day, but I never told anyone because I didn't know what to do. I had no idea what to expect or how to handle labor. And I was nervous because I had seen another one of the women hemorrhaging when she had her child. It was so bad, she had to be taken to the hospital, and I don't know what happened to her. So I suffered in silence, terrified and in pain.

Finally, one of the other women realized that I was in labor. She told the night nurse, who then called me in the labor room around eleven p.m. Giving birth was extremely difficult for me, as it is for so many women their first time. I had never known such pain before, and no one had explained to me what to do. I was given no instructions, no advice on how to breathe or how to push. I writhed in agony, without any family or friends present to comfort me. I remember begging for medication because the pain was so intense. The nurse came over and told me they couldn't give me any more pills.

By the time the doctor came, I'd been in labor so long and the baby's head was so large that I had begun to tear. The doctor decided to cut me so that I wouldn't tear anymore. No wonder I was in such agony. But my precious little child was born, and I found out it was a boy! He was eight pounds, ten ounces, and quite healthy. The date was July 21, 1959—a day I'll never forget as long as I live.

I wanted to see my little baby boy, to hold him, to study him and see who he looked like—Ernie or me. But the nurse wouldn't give him to me. In those days, they didn't allow the mother to see their baby or hold it if the child was being given up for adoption. I suppose they felt that made things easier on everyone, but for me, it was devastating.

The one thought I had at the time, the one hope, was that I could give him a name. And I had decided the perfect name for him. His father's middle name. *Nelson*. I'd thought at first about naming him Ernie Jr., but I realized that if I did, someone might guess who the father was. And I didn't want Ernie to get in trouble with the Marines. That's how naïve I was. I didn't even know that Nelson would get a new name from his adopted parents. No one would care what I had named him.

After I delivered my baby and I was in the recovery room, I woke up and saw my ten-year-old friend sitting beside me and holding my hand. She knew I had no family and wanted to be there for me when I woke up. But also, she was scared and wanted to know what to expect when she went into labor. I was glad to be able to share that with her. I finally found friends in the unwed mothers' home who truly cared about each other—and me.

But still, I had decisions to make about my future.

Throughout my time at the home, even after I gave birth, I debated what I would finally do. Despite all my family's threats and ultimatums, I desperately wanted to keep this darling little boy that God, Ernie and true love had given to me. I wanted to keep my baby because I loved Ernie and I knew we could make it work if we were just given a chance. But he couldn't get back to me, and my family was gone, and I was alone and without any other help to be found.

So while I wanted to keep little Nelson and raise him, in my heart I just knew I couldn't do it. It wouldn't be fair to him. I couldn't provide for him the way he deserved to be cared for. I loved him so much, and I wanted him to have the best of everything. My current situation made it impossible for me to take care of him. So I reluctantly admitted to myself that I needed to give him up for adoption after all.

As I recovered from giving birth, I still wasn't allowed to see my son. The staff at the home told me my baby would be leaving for his new home in two weeks, as soon as all the paperwork was finalized. Soon, the social worker came to see me. She had documents for me to sign, and while I sat there, she asked me questions about my family history so she could note anything of importance in her files.

I fought back tears as she asked me several questions. "Is the child a love baby?" she asked.

"Yes."

"I see. And where did you live?"

"My dad worked at Westminster College, and so did my mother and sister. They're in California now. That's where I'll go, after we're done here."

The woman made notes in her files. For a while, I was quiet, watching her work. But finally, I gathered up enough nerve to ask the biggest question on my mind.

"What's going to happen to my baby? Who is taking him in? What are they like? Are they a good family? Will he—will he be loved and cared for?"

The social worker nodded, as though she were not surprised in the least that I would ask this. She was very kind as she explained to me what would happen to little Nelson. She told me the couple adopting my son were very nice, loving and responsible people with a good income. They lived in New Castle, Pennsylvania, and they were unable to have children of their own. The husband was a respectable banker, and the wife was a competent homemaker. They would give my son the best life he could ever have. And they would absolutely love him.

I almost broke down into tears right then. My heart was breaking into tiny little shards. But I knew I couldn't give my beautiful little baby boy, my darling Nelson, the life he should have. With shaking fingers, I signed the adoption papers. And then I looked down at my lap, crushed. And at this point, I couldn't stop the tears from flowing down my cheeks.

The social worker saw how upset I was, and suddenly, she took pity on me. I can only explain what she did as a miracle of God's mercy toward me. The woman reached for my hand and spoke to me gently.

"You know, we're not supposed to do this, and I've never done it before," she said softly. "But if you would like to, you can put your maiden name on the top of the adoption papers."

She pointed to a small blank space with room enough for me to write. "If you put your name there, then if your son ever wants to find you, he'll have your name to work with. He'll know who the birth mother is. I'll even turn around so I can't see you do it. That way, if anyone asks, I can say I never saw you do it."

The woman didn't have to say it twice. I jumped at the chance, hoping and praying that someday I would see my baby boy again. Carefully, I wrote my last name down where she suggested I put it.

"Thank you," I said through tears. The social worker gave me a kind smile, and sent me on my way.

Soon, the two-week waiting period was over, and the social worker came to pick my son up. Though I was not supposed to see my baby after he was born, I was given an opportunity to see my tiny little boy, and I was so grateful and so full of sadness at the same time. The social worker told me I could dress him and handed me the baby clothes she had with her. That way, I could say goodbye.

Walking into the room where little Nelson lay in his crib, I carefully studied him. It was the first—and last—time I would get to see my baby. He was absolutely beautiful—with curly black hair like his father. I was supposed to dress him quickly, but I wanted to have as much time as I possibly could with this precious child of mine, so I moved slowly. I looked over every inch of him, counting his fingers and toes, trying to memorize every feature of his face before I had to hand him over again.

I must have lingered too long, because the social worker came in and took my little boy from me. As I stood there, she quickly finished dressing him and walked hurriedly down the hall. I followed her down the hall, and when I couldn't go any further, I went to the window and watched her take him out the door, down the steps and to a waiting car.

She was taking him away from me.

Broken in heart and spirit, I slid down the wall to the floor and cried my eyes out for at least an hour. As I wept, I prayed a desperate prayer that day, one that I would never forget—and God didn't either.

"Please, God," I begged as I sobbed unconsolably, "please just let me know my son is going to be okay. Please let me know he's okay. Please…"

Eventually, one of my friends came and got me and made me go to bed, where I finally cried myself to sleep. Two days later, my case worker took me to the airport and put me on a plane, heading to California. Mom, Dad, Donna and her husband, Richard, were all there waiting to pick me up. Though they must have seen how devastated I was, they never said a word.

Of all of them, only Donna seemed touched by what had happened. She had a one-year-old child of her own, and I suppose that she felt for me, because she was weeping. From then on, she would help me out when she could, as though trying to make up for her part in what had happened.

But my parents never spoke about the pregnancy or my baby ever again. They never even asked me if I'd had a boy or girl. Their refusal to acknowledge it made my loss even greater.

For years afterward, I held it against Mom that she, in particular, had forced this whole situation on me. She was a mother, after all, like I was. Surely, she could imagine the pain of giving up a child, just as Donna could. But my mother never, ever mentioned my baby. I couldn't forgive her for it.

I couldn't forgive myself either.

Eventually, I wrote Ernie a letter telling him we had a boy, and explaining that he had been adopted by a loving couple who were giving him a good home. Ernie called me from his military base.

"I'm going to get leave somehow," he insisted. "I'll come home, we'll get married, and we'll get our boy back."

Though I loved him for that, I told him no. "I can't take him away from the family that adopted him," I said. "It wouldn't be fair to anyone. But if you get leave and want to come back to see if you can still love me after all this, then I'll be here. We can get married and have another baby of our own."

I hoped Ernie would come back for me, because I still loved him. But he never did. He got very ill around that time, and ended up stuck on base for a long time. We never got connected again.

And again, I was alone.

But nearly every day for twenty-seven years, I prayed the same prayer I had made when my baby was taken away. "Please, Lord, let him be happy and healthy. And please let me know he's okay."

CHAPTER FIVE

Looking for Love in All the Wrong Places

After arriving in California in August 1959, I knew I had to somehow put my life back together. Since I had worked for IBM in Ohio, I decided to try my luck and so I went to the IBM office in San Diego. Fortunately, they had job openings to fill, and I had a good track record from my time in their Youngstown office. After reviewing my application and getting references from my previous coworkers, the San Diego office hired me. Having a job to go to every day was a good distraction. I was able to earn some money, and I even made a few friends at the office.

For a while, I lived with my parents. They had purchased a beautiful, large house that overlooked the Pacific Ocean, and there was plenty of room for me to stay there. Though I was still angry at my mother, I had nowhere else I could go. So I spent most of my time living day to day, going to work and coming home, and sometimes going to a movie with a friend. I still felt so lonely. I missed my little boy and Ernie. I tried to put them in the past and move on, but it was so hard.

The summer and fall sped by, and soon it was the holiday season. Christmas was about a month away when my brother Bill came home one day and made an announcement. San Diego was a military town, with U.S. naval and Marine bases in the area. Bill had seen a billboard that encouraged local families to invite a sailor home for Christmas dinner. He loved the idea and told us we should do it. My parents agreed, and Bill brought home a young sailor named Wally.

I found out later that Bill was gay. He had met this young man at a gay bar and was interested in him. But at the time, I didn't know this. I assumed Wally was simply a friend of Bill's, and since he kept coming by the house, I began to get to know him. We enjoyed each other's company and we started dating. I'm sure he was relieved to have a girlfriend to help protect his secret, because if he had been discovered, he would have been dishonorably discharged from the military. So, he had a lot to hide.

At the time, though, I didn't know any of this. Wally seemed like a perfect companion for me, and I was grateful to have someone's company and feel a little less lonely. Wally and I loved to dance, go to the beach, and talk. I told him many things about myself, but I never told him about my son. And obviously, there were things he didn't tell me either.

As we dated, we did experience a few hiccups that in hindsight, I can see now were warning signs. But I was so naïve and sheltered that I didn't recognize them. I remember one time in particular that Wally and I went to a bar in downtown San Diego that I'd never visited before. The place sure seemed strange to me, but I couldn't put my finger on exactly what was wrong. It was dark, and the people who sat together at the tables looked odd to me somehow.

I decided to visit the ladies room, and as I walked down a narrow hall, I noticed couples nearby who didn't look right—men with men, women with women. When I emerged from the ladies room, I ran into a woman who began talking to me. After a short time, I realized that she was making a pass at me. I was horrified! Quickly, I hurried back to where Wally waited for me, chatting with another young man. As soon as they saw me, they stopped talking and stared at me.

"I want to go home," I demanded.

"But we haven't been here that long," Wally argued.

"I've been here long enough. I'm ready to leave," I insisted.

Wally didn't look too pleased, but he got up and we left. I had no idea what was happening in that bar, and I didn't want to know.

Eventually, Wally proposed to me, and for a brief moment, it seemed as if my life would get back on track and I would have the loving husband and children I so desperately longed for. We got married in the Navy Chapel, a charming little building with beautiful wooden pews and beams on the ceilings, stained glass and candles. My parents were delighted to see me married, and I was too.

Wally was stationed in San Diego as a corpsman in the Naval hospital, which meant that we were able to stay near my family. We moved into a little apartment not far from my parents' home. For a while, everything was perfect. I was able to start making my own home, enjoyed Wally's company, and worked at IBM. And I prayed that God would give me another child.

Two months later, I got pregnant. I was so happy because I believed it was a sign that God had seen my loneliness, answered my prayers, and gave me another chance to be a mother. Finally, I was building a family of my own—or so it seemed.

That day, my sister and I were going to my mother's to help her clean and do some projects around the house, and Wally came with us. I was so thrilled to be pregnant again that I couldn't keep the news to myself any longer. I decided to share it with Wally and the family. So when we had a moment together, I told him the good news.

"Guess what, Wally? We're having a baby!"

The excitement I expected him to feel never appeared. Instead, he grew sullen and wouldn't speak to me. Not a word. I couldn't believe it.

"Wally, what is it? What's wrong?" I asked.

Instead of answering me, Wally stormed off. I stood there, shocked and dismayed. But I tried to reason with myself that it was all going to be fine somehow. "He's just surprised," I told myself. "He'll be back soon, and it'll be okay."

Soon, someone came to find me, but it wasn't Wally. My sister Donna was there to see me. She sat me down and said she wanted to talk with me.

"I'm sorry to have to be the one to tell you this, but Wally doesn't want children," she said.

I stared at her in complete disbelief. What husband didn't want to have children? And why was he talking to Donna instead of to me?

"He never said anything like that to me," I said. "I'm sure he's just surprised. I got pregnant so fast that he wasn't expecting to hear the news, that's all. I'm sure he'll come around after he's had a chance to get over the shock of it."

Donna shook her head. "I don't think so. Wally told me he doesn't want children. He's never wanted children. He was absolutely adamant about it." She paused for a second, then added reluctantly. "He's not happy about it. I guess his doctor told him he could never have any children, so he wasn't worried about it. Now it's happened, and he is miserable."

I was stunned and humiliated by what my sister was saying. Wally had never said a word to me about not wanting children. And he'd certainly never had the courtesy to tell me he believed he couldn't have children. If he had been right about that, we would have been childless. I would have been heartbroken about it, and I'm sure I would have blamed myself for it. I wondered how he could do such a thing to me.

Nevertheless, in spite of Wally's reaction, I knew in my heart that God was giving me a second chance to have a baby. And this time, I wasn't giving this baby up as I had given up my firstborn son. No one was going to make me have an abortion or give up another child to adoption.

Not even Wally.

In spite of how he felt about the baby, Wally didn't pressure me to give it up or abort it. Instead, he just stayed away from me as much as he could. I felt lonely and abandoned, but I focused on my unborn child. I had to be strong for the baby I was going to raise. So I kept trying to convince myself that everything would work out once the baby was born.

We needed extra money since we were about to have another mouth to feed, so Wally got a second job as an Arthur Murray dance teacher. I continued to work at IBM up until my ninth month. We saw little of each other because he worked nights and would come home late.

One night, he brought home a friend after work, and I could hear them talking in the living room. At nine months pregnant, I was thirsty a lot and needed to get something to drink, so I went out to the kitchen. As I did, I was shocked to see Wally and his friend—another man—kissing one another in the act of making love. The glass of water fell out of my hands. I ran back to the bedroom in hysterics.

As I lay on the bed, my face buried into a pillow, I heard the bedroom door open and close shut. It was Wally. He had sent his friend home, and now he wanted to talk with me—to explain himself, I suppose, or to try to pretend I was mistaken about what I'd seen. I was crying so hard that I couldn't look him in the eye.

"Will you quit it?" he demanded. When I kept crying, he slapped me hard across the face.

I held my cheek, glaring at him. "How dare you?" I demanded. I swore to myself right then and there that I'd never let him, or anyone else, slap me that way again.

He kept trying to convince me to calm down, that it was all nothing to worry about. But I wouldn't listen. "I'm leaving and going to my sister's place," I told him. "Don't try to stop me."

I grabbed a few things and left, and I stayed with Donna for a week. Every day was bringing me closer to my due date, and I was supposed to deliver the baby at the hospital where Wally worked. I didn't know what I was going to do, but I didn't want to see Wally again.

Finally, he called me and insisted I come back to the apartment.

"I will not," I said.

He threatened me. "If you don't come back, I'll make sure you can't deliver this baby at the Navy hospital. Where will you go then? Who's going to take you in? Who's going to pay for the birth?"

I'm sad to say his threats worked. I had no way to pay for the birth by myself. Needless to say, I went back to our apartment and stayed there with him until the baby was born. Like everything else that was happening in my life at the time, even the birth was difficult.

I went to the Navy hospital as soon as I went into labor, but the rooms were full so I had to wait in the hallway. Then they got me into a bed, but they left me alone to do other things. I lay there, having strong, quick contractions. The pain was intense. I cried out for someone to help me. The corpsmen were in another room watching TV, as if they didn't care what happened to me. But eventually, someone came to check on me.

He examined me and said, "That baby's head is crowning. I guess you'd better cross your legs."

Can you imagine? As if that was going to help me hold off the birth until they found me a room! But the doctor finally came in to help me get ready for the birth. They put a mirror up so I could watch the delivery, but soon took it away. I couldn't understand why until after my baby boy was delivered safely. I asked the doctor why I didn't get to see the delivery, and he told me the cord was wrapped around the baby's neck and they didn't want me to panic and see what was happening.

I named my newborn son Mark—and he was so handsome. I admired his face, his hair, his ten fingers and ten toes, just as I had done with my beautiful firstborn son. I was elated to have a child of my own, one I could keep and care for and love. Mark was so beautiful that I even thought maybe Wally would change his mind about fatherhood once he saw him.

But all my wishing and praying was no good. Wally still wanted nothing to do with his child, or with me. While I stayed in our apartment, tending our son, Wally continued to go out to his dance studio. He kept staying out til all hours of the night, barely seeing me, barely talking with me.

The final straw was seeing the friend Wally had been fooling around with, his boyfriend, pulling into our apartment's parking space with a boat that they both liked to use out on the ocean. When I saw that man in the driver's seat and thought about Wally spending time with him instead of me, I decided I'd had more than enough drama with this man. I wasn't going to keep putting up with it, so I left again, taking my infant son Mark with me.

At this point, there was only one course of action I could take. I wanted a divorce. There was no way I could make things work with Wally, and at this point, I no longer wanted to try. Staying with him would be a terrible situation for Mark and me, and I desired a better life for myself and my baby than Wally could give us.

Wally and I agreed to meet at the apartment to discuss the terms of our divorce. When I got there, I knocked and knocked, but he wouldn't answer. Thinking this was strange since his car was there, I went around back. I couldn't see inside due to the curtains, but I could hear Wally snoring. I banged some more, but I couldn't wake him up. Worried, I went back to my parents' house and asked my father and brother to see if they could wake him up.

"Something's wrong," I insisted. "Would you please go and check on him?"

They came back about an hour later. "The ambulance is taking him to the Navy hospital right now," they said.

"What on earth happened?" I asked.

"He tried to commit suicide," they told me. It turned out they had been unable to wake him, and so they called the police. When the police entered the apartment, they found Wally unresponsive. And they called the ambulance to take him to the emergency room.

Well, I was shocked to say the least. I knew he'd been unhappy with me, but I hadn't realized how desperate he had become when I refused to stay with him. He was terrified of being found out as a gay man and dishonorably discharged from his post.

As we waited for news of his recovery, I learned many things about Wally that I hadn't known before. He'd been engaged to be married before he met me, but he broke it off. I don't know why, but I suspect it had to do with his preference for men. I also learned that as a child, he'd been in foster care and was eventually adopted, but his foster father had abused him. Wally had lived a hard life, and it was no longer surprising that he struggled so much. He needed a lot of help—and I couldn't give it to him.

Eventually, Wally recovered from his suicide attempt, but soon he had more trouble. He was arrested for writing bad checks. And he begged me to come back to him and cover what he owed, so that the judge would let him out. I refused. The Navy discharged him, and there was nothing more to be said between us.

We went our separate ways. I got a divorce, and although we had a child together, I didn't ask Wally for any child support or alimony. I didn't want to keep ties between us that would only cause me more pain. I just wanted my son, and I would support Mark myself.

A year later, I met Don one night while coming out of a drive-in restaurant. My friend and I were sitting next to his car when we noticed his license plate said *Ohio*. Since I was from Ohio, we started up a conversation with him about where in Ohio he came from. Mark and I were living with my parents at the time, trying to make ends meet until I could get out on my own and make a new life for us. I was still searching for love and acceptance.

As Don and I got to know each other, we discovered we had a lot in common, and he treated Mark like he was his father. Things seemed good, and I thought that this time, I had found someone who truly loved me and my son, Mark—someone who wanted to be with us.

Soon, though, I found out Don wasn't free to marry me, because he had a wife and two children back in Ohio. They were separated, but the divorce wasn't final yet. The reason he'd come to California was to get away from the children and his wife. We had to wait until his divorce was final before we could get married. But at the time, I didn't mind.

My parents didn't approve of him, just as they hadn't approved of Ernie. But I was determined to make things work with Don. We continued dating. Once again, I got pregnant and I was so happy. *This time*, I thought, *I have a loving man in my life who will be thrilled to have a child with me.*

But Don wasn't thrilled at all. If anything, he felt the total opposite of how I did. I quickly discovered he hadn't been honest with me during the time we were dating. He hadn't told me, but the truth was, he didn't want more children.

"That's why I left my first wife and moved away from Ohio to California," he told me. "I'm tired of kids. I don't want us to have a child. I want you to get rid of it."

Needless to say, I was crushed to hear him say this. The dream I'd hoped for—a loving husband, beautiful children, a family that wanted me—was again falling apart. We argued, and I begged Don to reconsider. But he was adamant that he would not have more children. And I was just as adamant that I was not giving up another baby. But I felt so lost and desperate that I didn't know what to do next.

At this time, Don was the manager of a carwash, and some of his employees included men who had family over the border in Mexico. He asked one of his workers to have his wife take me to Tijuana. There, a doctor would give me a shot that would cause me to abort the baby.

Reluctantly, I agreed to go, though I didn't want to. But I also didn't know how I could take care of a second child if Don refused to help me. So, I traveled with the employee's wife across the border into Tijuana, not knowing what to expect.

When we arrived at the doctor's office, I was immediately uncomfortable. The place was filthy, with a dirt floor and a dark, worn look that seemed inappropriate for a medical office. The doctor himself had on clothes that were stained and dirty. There was an old, ugly curtain hanging between the front entrance of the office and the exam table. Something was clearly wrong with the whole situation. Here I was, stuck in Tijuana with people I didn't know, and I was beginning to feel frightened.

Now, I didn't speak Spanish, and the carwash employee's wife didn't speak English, so I couldn't talk with her and share my concerns. To my great surprise, though, the doctor didn't speak English either. *What on earth is happening here?* I wondered. *Why has Don sent me here?*

The doctor led me into a room alone, and instructed me to get on the table. I assumed he was going to give me some kind of shot that would cause an abortion, and even though I didn't want to do it, I felt helpless to resist. It had taken so much out of me to stand up to my family when Scott was born. I didn't know how I could do it again. So I climbed up on the exam table and waited, shaking with fear and shame and grief.

The doctor studied me. But he didn't grab any of his medical equipment. Instead, he started to pull down his pants, and I realized he intended to force himself on me. I don't know if he thought this would abort the baby, or if he just wanted to take advantage of me since I had no one to protect me. But I began to scream at the top of my lungs, hollering for help.

The woman who had driven me to Tijuana heard me yelling. She came running into the room and got me out of there. Thank God for her! I don't know what awful things would have happened if she hadn't cared enough to help me.

After that episode, I didn't have any respect for Don, but I thanked God for our son, Ray. He was a beautiful boy, and I was grateful God gave him to me. After Ray was born, Don reluctantly married me, but sadly our relationship didn't last long.

For one thing, Don was not the kind person I had thought he was when we first met. I'd hoped that he would be good to his son, Ray, and my son, Mark. But he was angry, impatient and harsh with them. If they didn't respond the way he wanted them to, he would take out his anger on them. It was awful. Children should never be treated that way.

In addition, Don bounced from job to job, unable to hold onto his employment because he'd get caught stealing from his employers. It was terrible. He owed child support for his children in Ohio, but he couldn't—or wouldn't—pay it. Eventually, the police tracked him down. They warned Don that he had to take care of paying the child support he owed to his first wife, or he would go to jail. I ended up making his monthly child support to the court.

But he certainly didn't appreciate it. Instead, he started staying out all night. Then he stayed away from home for days. I had no idea what he was doing, while I was struggling to keep my job and care for my two young sons. Eventually, I realized he was seeing someone else while he was still married to me, which was apparently his pattern of behavior.

A few months later, I received a phone call from Don's girlfriend. She said, "I just wanted to let you know, I'm not sending Don's monthly child support to the court for his children from his first wife anymore, because I'm leaving him." Don had suckered that woman into giving him money to pay his child support too. Who knows if any of the money she or I gave Don ever went to his children?

I continued to try to make our marriage work somehow, but it was useless. I began to plan my second divorce, though it pained me to do so. The last straw came one Father's Day when Don actually showed up at home.

I'd been hoping he would come home for the boys' sake if not for mine, so I bought a sweater outfit for the boys to give him as a Father's Day present. I even cooked dinner so we could have a little time together for the sake of the children. Don came inside, took the present and opened it. He went into the bathroom, showered, shaved and cleaned up. He put on his new outfit.

And then he walked out the door, with barely a word for me or the boys, except to say that he couldn't stay for dinner because he had plans. It was heart-breaking and infuriating, all at once. But I didn't want the boys to feel too hurt by Don's behavior, so I decided to take them to my mother's house for dinner. That way, I could wish my father a happy Father's Day and try to pretend things were normal.

While driving, I spotted Don's car ahead of us. I pressed the gas pedal to the floor and sped up until I caught up to him. As I glanced into his car, I could see him sitting there with his girlfriend, pleased as punch at himself. He looked over and saw us.

"Wave to your father," I told Mark and Ray. We all waved at Don and his girlfriend, as if everything was fine.

But I was devastated.

When I arrived at my mother's house, I handed the boys off to her. "Take care of them," I pleaded, in tears. "I need some time to myself. I need to think."

She nodded and brought the boys inside. I got back in the car and drove around town, barely paying attention to where I was going. My eyes were filled with tears, so much so that the streets looked blurry. I was in hysterics, just feeling like I had no hope left in me for anything.

"I should just end it all," I told myself. And it sounded like a brilliant idea. No one wanted me. I couldn't seem to make my life work. And who would miss me? Maybe Mark and Ray would even be better off without me.

People think terrible things like this when they're broken-hearted and under pressure. I was no different. Killing myself seemed like it made sense. So, I got myself a bottle of sleeping pills and hopped back in the car, swallowing them as I drove around, still crying. At one point, I even stopped a phone booth to call my sister, Donna.

"Please take care of my boys," I begged her.

"Dixie, what's wrong?" she asked. "Where are you? What's happening?"

"Just take care of Mark and Ray," I insisted, before I hung up on her.

As I drove through the lonely streets, feeling utterly alone and helpless, I heard a voice inside my head. A thought.

"Pull over," the voice said.

I obeyed and brought the car to a stop. Looking around, I realized I had parked my car in a church parking lot. As I looked at the church's steeple and the cross atop it, the voice spoke to me again.

"Pray to God for help," it said.

Still in tears, I began to pray. "God, please help me and guide me." For I had lost all faith in my judgment and hope for happiness, and without Him, I had no chance at all. I sat in that car, in that parking lot, and prayed for a long time.

All at once, a sudden sense of peace overcame me. My heart told me that God loved me. And I knew I needed to stop thinking about suicide, go home and start building a life for me and my boys again.

Soon, I had moved back in with my parents again. I couldn't manage my old apartment on my salary alone, and I needed someone to help watch Mark and Ray while I worked. This time, though, I wanted to make better choices for myself and my sons.

I made a friend named Pat, who was also divorced and had two children that she was raising on her own. We became roommates and rented a house together. Our kids could play together, and we were able to support and encourage each other as single mothers. I felt I was getting a hold of myself. And it was good to have a friend standing with me as I started my life over again.

Pat and I started going to church too, and thanking God for all our blessings. I was soon ready to socialize with adults again, so I joined a singles bowling league, where I made a lot of friends. At last, I felt like

I was finding my way with being alone with my boys and away from my mom and dad. And it felt wonderful!

I bowled with the league for about a year when I met a man I liked on another team and started to date again. Doug was a chief in the Navy, divorced, and had a little girl. After a year of dating, he got orders to go to Rhode Island for sea duty. We decided to get married in December, and then we would leave in February for Rhode Island. This would give us time to enjoy married life for a bit before our big move.

Two weeks after we got married, Doug got an unexpected phone call from his first wife. She told him she was on drugs and couldn't handle their five-year-old daughter Tammy.

"If you don't take her, I'm going to put her up for adoption," she threatened.

Doug and I couldn't imagine allowing that to happen. So, we took Tammy in. In one day, Doug went from being single to a husband with a wife and three children, and I went from being single to being a wife with three children, quitting my good job and moving clear across the country to live in a place I'd never been, and where I didn't know anyone. It was not easy.

Shortly after we got to Rhode Island, Doug had to leave to catch his ship. I was left without a place to live and three kids to take care of on my own. Doug couldn't get paid until he reached his ship, which meant that money was tight too. With some of my savings, I paid the first month's rent for a cramped, one-bedroom cottage. Then I bought a triple bunk bed for the kids to sleep in, and placed it in the sunroom. The room was so small that the bed was the only thing that fit in there, and the kids had to crawl into bed at the room's opening.

After that, our furniture arrived. I had to put our storage boxes and everything else in the small fruit cellar because there wasn't time to unpack it all, and no other place to put it. A week later, it rained hard. When I went to the cellar to get some fresh clothes for the kids, I discovered the boxes floating! Everything was soaked. I wanted to cry.

During this time, I missed Doug so much. We couldn't even communicate because he was at sea, trying to catch up with the ship he was assigned to. Not only was I lonely, but he couldn't send us any money. And I didn't have any money left after paying for our rent and the children's bed. Sadly, I had to rob the children's banks in order to buy food.

Doug went on to serve in the Vietnam War, which meant I was alone for quite a long time while he was in the military. But during this time, I remembered how faithful God had been to me over the years. So I turned to Him again. I prayed hard, and God was right there with me, helping me to make the right decisions that would take care of me and the children.

Things got better. Doug finally got orders that brought us back to San Diego, where we remained until he retired. I was blessed with two handsome sons, Mark and Ray, whom I loved so much.

For the first time in my life, I wasn't afraid or lonely, because I felt God's presence with me. And soon enough, the miracle I'd been praying for would begin to come to pass in a way I never would have imagined.

Dixie Lee Barbe

Scott, Dixie and Ernie

Dixie's Parents and Grandparents

Dixie Lee Barbe 1940

Scott Edward Russell 1961

Christmas—the day Dixie & Scott's family met Ernie again

Dixie's home growing up

Scott and his two moms

Scott and Micah at Renewal Ranch

Reuniting- Mom and Son

Dr. Margo Bush the publisher,
Scott and Dixie

Where Dixie & Scott would go to talk with God

Dixie wins sweater queen

Dixie's Mom and Dad's wedding

Dixie L Brown

Scott walking Dixie down the aisle to marry Robert Brush

Dixie's wedding to Robert Brush

Ray, Dixie, and Mark 1966

Dixie's mom, dad, sister Donna and brother Donald at grandparents' home.

Mark and Ray (back row) with Scott and Dixie (front row)
The day Dixie had all three sons together for the first time.

CHAPTER SIX

A Name at the Top of the Adoption Papers

Over the years, I wondered how my son would ever find me if he chose to seek me out. In the closed adoptions of the 1950s, the birth mother wasn't allowed to reach out to her child directly. The birth mother's identity was kept a secret from their adopted child, and the adopted parents' identity was kept secret from the birth mother. It was thought that it would be a mistake to allow contact. And in many cases, the women who gave up their child for adoption wanted to close the chapter on that part of their life and never look back.

For me, though, I felt an aching loss at not being there to watch my firstborn son grow up. He was a missing part of my life that I always hoped to recover one day. Because my records with the adoption agency were sealed, there wasn't much I could do to reach out to my son directly. But there was one action I could take—so I did. I always kept my college listing up-to-date, making sure my latest address and telephone number were always available.

Remember, the social worker had allowed me to put my last name on the adoption paper, and it was the only lifeline I had to reach my son one day. If he had any chance of reaching out to me, it would have to be because he tracked me down by my maiden name. And the only place that still listed me by my maiden name was Westminster College. So, no matter where I moved or who I married, I was sure to let the college know how to find me.

It's a good thing I did this, because Scott's adopted mother, Marge, cleverly made use of it. In fact, I often think about the miracle that God did within Marge's heart that paved the way for Him to answer my prayers to know my son was alive and well and happy.

The miracle of restoration and reunion that God was carefully or-chestrating began right at the time Scott was born. When Marge first saw the adoption papers for the new baby boy that she and her hus-band, Ed, were taking into their little home, she noticed a word at the top of one of the pages. She puzzled over the letters.

Finally, she pointed to the scratched letters and asked the social worker, "What does this mean?"

The social worker said, "Oh, that's the name of the child's birth mother. No need to worry about that. Now, let's talk about what else you need to know before you take your new son home with you."

Something inside Marge told her she might want to know that name someday. Or if not her, then perhaps the beautiful baby boy with curly dark hair that she had already fallen in love with might one day want to know. Quickly and discreetly, she wrote down the name, my last name, so she would have it handy in the future.

I didn't know any of this at the time, but while I was living in California, going through so many trials and searching for love in all the wrong places, my firstborn son, Scott, was growing up a happy, healthy boy in New Castle, just ten miles from where I once lived in New Wilmington as a teenager.

Scott grew up the only son of a kind couple named Ed and Marge. They couldn't have children of their own, so they were delighted to give my little baby boy a happy, loving home. Over the years, Scott played sports and enjoyed his family and friends. He didn't know he was adopted at first.

When Scott was eight years old, Marge and Ed made a decision. They decided to tell Scott the truth about his birth, and that he was adopted. Later, when I finally met her, we talked about many things, but I never found out what drove her to share his adoption with him. Perhaps she thought he would find out somehow anyway, and she wanted to be the one to tell him. Or maybe, even then, God put it on her heart to do it, so that one day He could answer my prayers and let me know my son was alive and well.

I can only imagine the courage it took for Marge and Ed to reveal to Scott that he was adopted. After all, they must have wondered how their son would react. Would he be confused? Furious? Disappointed? Crushed? Would he reject them? Nevertheless, they shared the truth with him.

"Will you still be my parents?" Scott asked them. "Everything is going to be the same, right? You still love me, don't you?"

Marge and Ed must have been so relieved to hear him say that! "Yes, of course," they said. "We will always love you, and you will always be our son."

And that settled it. Scott went on about his activities, playing and enjoying life as eight-year-olds do. And he never gave his adoption another thought until he was in his twenties, when God began to put it on his heart to reach out to me.

During the time that Scott was growing up, I continued to do the one thing I could do—praying to know my son was okay. Days turned into months, months into years, and years into more than two decades.

Then one day, Doug and I began watching a movie on TV. It told the story of an unwed mother, much like me, who gave her son up for adoption and then tried to get him back. As I sat there, watching the woman's heartbreak, I found myself reliving my own past. I couldn't stop thinking about my time in the unwed mothers home over twenty years earlier. I remembered how hard it was to give my baby up for adoption. I remembered how much I wanted my own son back. Watching another mother's struggle, one so much like mine, hit me so hard that I started to cry.

I couldn't sit there, out in the open, so exposed—especially with my husband and sons sitting there, staring at me in confused shock. So I ran into the bedroom to sob in private.

A few moments later, Doug came into the bedroom. "Dixie, why are you crying?" he asked gently, and clearly concerned. "What on earth is wrong?"

Hesitantly, through my sobs, I admitted the truth to him. For the first time, I told someone what I had gone through as a young woman. "I have another son," I admitted, "a baby I had to give up for adoption."

Doug was stunned. I'd never told him any of this before, and it was news to him. I was so nervous, wondering what he would think of me. But he didn't judge me. Instead, he listened carefully and kindly as I explained how I'd become pregnant with my very first child, out of wedlock. And though I'd wanted to keep my son, it seemed impossible, so I was forced to give him up.

"I've been praying for him every day since he was born," I told Doug. "And I've been praying and praying that God would somehow let me know my little boy is all right."

Doug comforted me and encouraged me that day. But I still wanted to know my son was okay, and I continued to pray for him, just as I always had.

Later that month, I received in the mail a copy of Westminster College's newspaper. As I opened it and read it, I saw a picture of the college's football team, which had won the championship that year.

Something inside me told me my son might be in the picture. He'd be the right age to be a college student. And he had grown up in New Castle, near Westminster College, according to what the social worker had told me when I'd signed the adoption papers. In those days, people didn't move nearly as often as they do now. It was very likely that his parents still lived in New Castle, and even that Scott could be going to college at my alma mater.

It seemed like a long shot that I'd get a glimpse of him in the college's newspaper, but I knew anything was possible with God. What if my little boy, now grown up, had decided to go to Westminster? It was certainly possible. And his father, Ernie, had been so athletic. Perhaps our son was athletic too. All of this could be possible.

So, hoping against hope, I studied the picture of the football team for a long time. My eyes kept going back to one football player in particular, a tall and handsome young man with dark, curly hair. He reminded me of Ernie.

Could it be my son? I wondered.

Once again, I turned to God and shared my thoughts with Him, my fingers resting gently on the young man's face in the photograph. "Please just let me know if he made it and is okay," I prayed. "I won't interfere with his life. I just want to know if he is happy and well."

Meanwhile, Marge was secretly working to find out what she could about the birth mother whose name sat at the top of the adoption papers for her son, Scott. Years later, she told me that if she'd been in my shoes, she would have wanted to know what had happened to her son, and that's why she sought out my information to share with Scott. I'm convinced that God put this desire into Marge's heart so that I would one day have the answer to my prayers. And she faithfully went about her task of finding me.

Somehow, Marge learned that I had once attended Westminster College, probably because the social worker had told her a little about me, just as she had told me a little about the couple who were adopting my son. Armed with this knowledge and a last name scribbled in rough handwriting atop the adoption papers, Marge took a trip to Westminster College and visited the office where student and alumni records were kept.

An older woman smiled at her as she entered the records office. "May I help you?"

"I'm looking for someone," Marge said. She must have been nervous, but perhaps she was excited too. And certainly, she was full of courage! "I believe this young woman lived here in New Wilmington, and maybe attended college here. Have you ever heard of someone by the name of Barbe?" she asked, giving them my maiden name.

To her surprise, the older woman behind the counter nodded immediately. "Oh, yes!" She smiled. "Yes, I certainly do remember them. The father, Professor Barbe, was a professor of speech and dramatics here, and quite popular. His wife worked in the administration office here, and I worked with her."

"Do you know if they had a daughter?"

"Oh, yes, they had two daughters—Donna and Dixie. Both attended college here, as I recall."

This was wonderful news to Marge's ears, and she leaned in toward the other woman, smiling back at her. "I'm looking for one of the girls." She paused, considering what to say next, because she needed information but she wanted to be discreet about it. "I believe the daughter I'm looking for would have graduated around 1958 perhaps? She'd be around fifty now, I think."

"Ah, then you're talking about the younger one, Dixie. She was several years younger than her sister, as I recall."

"Do you have an address for Dixie? Or a phone number, or any other way I might be able to reach her?"

The woman studied Marge, and then asked, "May I inquire as to why you're looking for her?"

Should I tell her? Marge wondered. She decided to be discreet. "My family is connected with hers," she finally said. "And I just don't know how to get in touch with her. I was hoping you might help."

The woman behind the counter nodded in understanding. "I see. Well, you know, we always wondered what happened to them too. The family was here one day as always, and then they were gone so suddenly. They left in the middle of the night, it seemed. No one ever knew where they went, or why."

Marge shrugged, not wanting to say anything that might cause my family trouble. After all, in a small town, scandals never die. She chose to help keep my secret. "Well, I'm sure it was all harmless enough. But I do appreciate your helping me."

"Of course! I'm happy to help." The woman wrote down my name and telephone number on a slip of paper, and handed it to Marge. "Good luck reaching out to her," she said. "I hope it goes well."

For a while, Marge kept my information to herself, waiting for the right time to share it. Finally, on Mother's Day, she decided it was time. Scott was about to turn twenty-seven years old. That day, he came to visit his mother and celebrate this special day with her, just as he'd always done.

"Hi, Mom. You're looking beautiful, as always!" Scott gave her a hug and a kiss, and handed her a card. "Happy Mother's Day!" Little did he know that the course of his life was about to change.

"Scott, I have something to give you," Marge said as they sat in the home's cozy living room.

Scott laughed. "Mom, today is Mother's Day! I'm the one who's supposed to be giving you gifts, remember?"

Marge nodded, but she didn't waver. "I know, but I'm doing it anyway. This is for you," she said. And she handed him a slip of paper.

Puzzled, Scott stared at the piece of paper, then looked up at his mother. She sat there calmly, a tender smile on her face. "Mom, what is this?"

Marge had a twinkle in her eye. "It's your birth mother's name and telephone number," she said.

It was not what Scott was expecting. Not at all. He sat there, staring at the paper, and then staring at his mother. "I don't understand, Mom. Why are you giving this to me?"

"It's Mother's Day. And I just think it would be good for you to have this. One day you might want to speak with her, and when you do, you'll have her number."

"But you're my mother. I don't even know her."

"I know, Scott, I know." Marge squeezed her son's hand gently. "You will always be my son, and I will always love you and have a place for you in my life. But trust me, this information is something you should have handy, in case you ever want it. As a mother, I know how important you are to me. And so..."

She gave a little shrug. "Every mother wants to know their child is okay. One day, maybe you'll get the chance to tell her how much you love her."

"Ok, Mom. I hear you. Thank you for sharing this with me." With a shrug of his own, Scott put the piece of paper in his pocket and continued his visit with Marge, giving little thought to the name and telephone number he now had in his possession. He had no intention of doing anything with it, but he wasn't about to tell that to Marge.

A few months went by. And while I continued to live my life as I always had, I never forgot the young man whose face I had seen in that college football photo. *Could it be my son? And if not, where was my son? When would God answer my prayer?*

One day, my situation suddenly turned around. It happened so fast that, looking back now, I just know it had to be God orchestrating it all. The phone in my home began to ring.

Who could that be? I wondered. I wasn't expecting any calls, and Doug wasn't either. *How strange!*

When I answered the call, a young man's voice came over the phone line. "Hello," he said. "Is Dixie there?"

"Yes, this is Dixie," I answered.

On the other end of the line, the young man sounded nervous. But he pressed on and told me something utterly incredible.

"I'm not trying to cause you any problems or upset your life in any way," he explained, pouring out the words in a torrent. "But I was praying one night, and I felt really strongly that I was supposed to call you and let you know I'm all right."

For a moment, I couldn't even imagine what was happening. In fact, the young man hadn't even given me his name. Was it a prank call? "Who is this?" I asked.

There was a brief pause on the other end, a moment of total quiet. And then the young man said calmly, "I'm your son, Dixie. My name is Scott. Today is my birthday, and God told me to call you on my birthday, so you would know it was really me."

I glanced at the calendar out of habit, though I knew exactly what day it was. July 21. My firstborn son's birthday. I wanted to believe it was him. But even though I'd been praying for this day to come, I couldn't quite imagine how it could all be true. So I said the only thing I could think of.

"How do you know you're my son?"

As I listened in amazement, the young man, Scott, told me everything he knew about his adoption. He explained how his mother, Marge, had seen my last name at the top of his adoption papers, and how she had asked the social worker what it meant. He told me how she had tracked my contact information down at Westminster College and given it to him so that he could call me when he was ready to reach out to me.

I felt tears coming to my eyes. *No*, I thought, *I need to listen! I need to ask...* But as Scott told me his story, I became overwhelmed with emotion. God had answered my prayer after twenty-seven long years. Suddenly, I began to sob, uncontrollably, to the point that I couldn't talk.

"Dixie, are you ok?" Scott asked.

But I just couldn't get any words out through my tears.

"I tell you what," he said. "Here's my phone number. Call me back anytime you're ready to talk. There's no rush. I'll be here for you anytime."

After we hung up, I cried hard. I knew he had to be my son, because he'd used the exact words I'd be praying to God for so long. I was elated, excited—and so nervous too. *What should I do next?* I wondered. I needed time to gather myself together.

Soon, Doug came in and found me in tears. Again, he found himself asking me what had happened. This time, I had good news to share. I told him my son had called me to let me know he was ok. Doug was as surprised as I had been when I answered the phone. And he was so happy for me.

"What did you talk about? What did you say to him?" he asked.

"I was crying so hard, I couldn't talk," I said. "I had to hang up the phone."

"What? Dixie, for goodness' sake, call him back. Right now!"

As Doug and I spoke about the situation, I mentioned that my high school reunion was happening soon, and I wanted to attend. It would be a perfect time to meet Scott.

"Would that be ok?" I asked.

"Of course," Doug said. "Do it!"

"What if I can't get the time off from work?"

"Just explain to your boss what's happening. I'm sure she will understand. How could she not let you go?"

"But I'll need to get plane tickets. I don't know…"

"Dixie!" Doug squeezed my hand, smiling at me. "We'll make it happen. Just do it."

Doug was right, and I knew it. I had to go and meet Scott. And if God had arranged for him to reach out to me, then God would work all the other details out for me too. First, I went to my boss and explained my story to her. She cried along with me and told me to take the time off I needed and go to Pennsylvania.

Then I called Scott. "I'm sorry I couldn't talk to you more when you first called," I explained. "I was crying so hard because I have been praying for twenty-seven years that God would let me know you're all right. And now I know, and I am so grateful!"

"Me too," Scott said. "In fact, I'm glad you called back. I wasn't sure if I had maybe upset you with my call."

"Oh, no, I wasn't upset. Just overwhelmed. I'm so thrilled to hear from you." We talked for a while, and then I told him I had a class reunion coming up. "I would love to meet you. If that would be ok with you, that is."

"Absolutely! I'd love that," Scott said.

Now, there was just one last thing to do before I left—and that was to talk with my two other sons, Mark and Ray. *How would they react?* I wondered. I'd never told them I'd had a child that I gave up for adoption, and I wasn't sure what they would think of me when they found out. *Would they be disappointed in me? Would they be hurt in some way?* That was the last thing I wanted.

I sat both Mark and Ray down with me and explained to them what had happened to me so many years ago. I explained they had an older brother, and I had a chance to finally meet him. When I finished my story, both boys stood up and gave me a hug and a kiss. I'll always remember what Mark said to me that day too.

"Mom, no matter what your past is, I'll always love you."

Tears came to my eyes, yet again. The love I'd been longing for from men all these years, the love I tried to find in all the wrong places, was now here in front of me. It was in my two sons. And now, I was about to meet my third son. What an amazing miracle!

Soon enough, I boarded a plane and headed to Pennsylvania—scared, happy, excited, worried about hurting Marge, and wondering how everything would turn out.

CHAPTER SEVEN

A Life Redeemed

During the twenty-seven years that I had been trying to figure out my path in life, and praying for God to give me peace about my firstborn son's welfare, Scott was growing up just ten miles away from where I'd grown up. His parents, Marge and Ed, raised him in the lovely little town of New Castle, Pennsylvania. It's in the far western part of the state, near the border with Ohio, just several miles away from Youngstown where the Florence Crittendon home was located.

Where Scott was born.

New Castle has a charming, historic, small town feel. And Scott's parents had good jobs, so he was raised in an environment that gave him many opportunities for success. Though he learned that he was adopted at age eight, he didn't think much about it at the time. He was secure in the knowledge that Marge and Ed loved him, and as a young boy, that was all he needed at the time.

But as he grew up, Scott began to wonder more about himself and his birth parents. He found himself grappling with many questions that adopted children face, questions no one could answer for him.

He'd look in the mirror, studying his dark, curly hair and dark eyes, so different from how Marge and Ed looked. *Do I look like my parents?* he asked himself. *Who do I take after? I wonder who I got the dark tan from.*

As he played baseball, basketball and football with his school friends, excelling at athletics, he found himself wondering about his abilities. *Who did I get my athletic ability from? Is one of my parents good at sports too? Would I have been coached by them? What would they think about my success on the field?*

Scott also began to have doubts about himself—the same kinds of questions we all face as young people. But it can be worse when a person is adopted, because there is the added pressure of having questions about your past that your adopted parents can't tell you.

Why did things happen the way they did? he asked himself, over and over, as a teenager. *Why was I given up for adoption, when everyone else I know grew up with their real parents? Is there something wrong with me?*

It would be years later before I could tell him the truth—there was nothing wrong with him. Nothing at all. He was beautiful and perfect in my eyes, and in God's eyes. He was always, always loved. And if I could have done so, I would have kept him in a heartbeat.

When Scott was a senior in high school, his father Ed suddenly died. It was a terrible time, traumatic and heartbreaking. He and Ed had been close, so he took his father's death very hard. Like many people in similar circumstances, Scott began to blame God for taking his father away from him. And as a result, he began to rebel against anything godly in his life.

"That's when I truly began to struggle with the questions I had about who I was, the adoption, and everything else I couldn't understand about life," Scott eventually told me, years later. "I was so angry at God for what I saw as His decision to take my dad from me, that if I thought God wanted me to do something, I did the opposite."

After Ed died, Scott began to spin out of control. He began taking risks, such as drinking and taking drugs, but he managed to graduate high school with a decent grade point average. With his athletic skills and his GPA, he was able to attend Westminster College, the same college I had attended two decades earlier. He walked the same halls that my brother, sister and I had walked, and visited the same offices where my parents had once worked. He played football there, for the same team I had been a cheerleader for. And he did it all without having any idea of the connection our family had to the college.

During Scott's college years, he was rowdy. Often, he would court trouble, and he has told me that he even came close to ending his life. But looking back now, it seems as if God always kept an eye on him. Perhaps my prayers helped to protect Scott from danger. If it wasn't for God's intervention, he probably would not be here right now.

One story Scott told me about his college days is a perfect example of how God is faithful to watch over us, especially when someone has been praying for us. Here's what he shared with me:

"One of my teammates and I were driving around, pretty drunk, after we had been bar hopping," Scott said to me. "We were driving his orange Volkswagen on the sidewalk of the quad in the center of the college campus. We finally stopped at the three-story science lab, got out of the car, and pulled the building's fire escape down so we could climb onto the slate roof. Our plan was to walk across the roof and climb in a different window. It's the kind of alcohol-induced prank that college students are fond of pulling.

"It was three o'clock in the morning, so there was a lot of dew on the roof. But we didn't realize it. So I tried to walk across the slate shingles, and suddenly I found myself sliding down the steep roof like I was on a sheet of ice. I was very much in danger of slipping to the ground—a three-story fall that could cause serious injuries. I realized I had just one chance to catch myself, which was to catch hold of the gutter. As I reached for it, I pushed it out of alignment, away from me, and missed my chance to grab it.

"I remember thinking, I can't believe I'm falling off this roof. But I did. I hit the ground butt first, and then my face hit the ground. I collapsed like a pancake. I thought I was going to die. From the rooftop, my teammate was calling my name and asking if I was ok.

"I realized I had not died, and in fact, I wasn't hurt badly either. It was a miracle. I called out to him: 'I'm ok.'

"He yelled back, 'Hey, where are your pants?'

"I looked down and saw that my pants were gone. I don't know how it happened, but there I was, in my underwear. I looked around. No pants on the ground. Then, I slowly looked up and there they were—stuck and hanging from the roof. I wasn't going to go back up to get them, was I? So I left them there and went back to my dorm room. The incident made the college newspaper the next day. 'Whose pants are these?' said the headline."

Scott and I still laugh at that story—but it's serious too, because he could have been injured badly in a fall from the roof that night. Yet he wasn't hurt, and we believe it is the goodness of God that saved him and protected him. When people pray, God begins working in so many ways to bring about the answers. I'd prayed to know Scott was ok, which meant Scott would need to be ok. And I believe God protected him for that reason.

As Scott grew older, God continued to work in his life. His presence was there, watching over my son, even while he was drinking, taking drugs, living a rebellious lifestyle and putting himself at risk. He even came close to ending his life. He would drive his candy apple red, white convertible top, GTO sports car over a hundred miles per hour, contemplating letting it skid off the road because he was experiencing so much pain and grief over the loss of Ed and his unanswered questions about why his parents gave him up for adoption.

Thankfully, God intervened in a major way to turn his life around before it was too late.

When Scott was twenty-two years old, a female coworker invited him to church. She had a daughter and thought Scott might be interested in meeting her. So he agreed to go to church.

That day, as he sat in the pews and listened to the minister preach, the message spoke to him. He realized that God loved him and had a plan for him. And when the minister asked people to invite God into their hearts, Scott responded. He asked the Lord to forgive him, come into his life and change him. Scott went from spiritual death to life that day.

It was not too long after he gave his life to God that Scott met his future wife, Amy. They met in church, and thirty days later, Scott asked Amy to marry him. His life took a new path, a blessed path. He left behind his rebellious ways and walked in a new peace he'd never had before. He and Amy had two children, Marcus and Micah. The couple has made, and continues to make, a great difference in the lives of those they meet.

None of these things would have happened if I had not chosen life when I was pregnant with him. I'm so grateful I chose life back then, even though it was hard to do so. Seeing Scott and his wonderful family has made that decision completely worthwhile and beautiful to both of us.

Five years after Scott gave his life to God, things began to fall into place that would bring him and me together. As I've said, his mother Marge was working to find out how to reach me, and then she gave him my contact information. But Scott wasn't interested at first in meeting me. In fact, he put my contact information in a drawer and forgot about it...until God brought it back to his memory and spoke to him about me.

Scott's twenty-seventh birthday began to draw near. One day, as he was praying, God began to speak to him about calling me.

"Call Dixie," that inner voice said to him. "Call your birth mother on your birthday, and let her know that you are all right."

Scott didn't know what to think at first. "Are you sure, Lord?" he prayed.

The more he asked the Lord about it, the more certain he became that God wanted him to call me. But it was an uncomfortable situation. He couldn't imagine what it would be like to talk with me. What if I didn't want to hear from him? What if I told him he was a mistake? What if calling me opened up old wounds?

"As soon as I decided to call her, I had reasons not to do it," he later told me. "I knew I was probably a skeleton in her closet. I thought she might have forgotten me. And by calling her, I might be stirring up all kinds of trouble for both of us."

But he felt certain that God wanted him to do it, so he made up his mind to obey. As nervous as he was, he made the call that brought us together again, finally, after so many years had passed by.

And because he obeyed the Lord, a miracle was about to take place. An answer to a decades-long prayer was coming into existence.

Soon, I was on a plane heading to Pennsylvania, ready to meet him and see what the Lord was about to do in both of our lives. I was nervous and excited, and so was he. And even in our reunion, the hand of God was evident.

CHAPTER EIGHT

Hugging the Bag Lady

When I got off the plane in Pittsburgh, I was a bundle of nerves. It had been a week since I'd first heard from Scott. What would it be like to see him in person? Would I even recognize him?

Would he forgive me for giving him away?

There was only one way to find out. I got into the car I'd rented and drove to New Castle. Scott had offered to pick me up, but I thought it was best for me to have my own car. I'd planned to attend my class reunion, and the car would give me freedom to come and go as I pleased. And it would also be less awkward for me to have my own transportation if my meeting with Scott didn't go as smoothly as I was hoping. There would be no pressure on him to drive me around if he somehow didn't like me or didn't feel comfortable with me.

As I drove on roads I hadn't traveled upon in years, I couldn't help wondering if things would go ok when I met Scott. The familiar trees and buildings of Pennsylvania that I'd grown up knowing were all around me, and so were the memories of what had happened to me all those years ago. I prayed during my drive, and followed the directions to New Castle. But as soon as I arrived at the town mall, I realized I didn't know what to do next.

So, I parked the car and phoned Scott from inside the mall. (Back in those days, public telephones were everywhere, so this was easy.) As it turned out, Scott had been waiting anxiously for me to call. He was concerned that I had gotten lost. So when he answered the phone and heard my voice, he was so relieved.

"I'm in New Castle at a little mall, and I can't go any further," I told him. "I don't know where you are or how to find you." As I described my surroundings, Scott recognized where I was.

"I know exactly where you are," he said. "I'll meet you at the payphones. Just wait for me. I'll be there soon."

As we hung up, I could feel butterflies forming in my stomach. To calm myself and give myself something to do, I stepped into a store near the phone bank. That way, I could look around the store and keep myself occupied while I waited for my son to arrive.

At a time like this, it's natural to have all kinds of questions going through your mind, wondering how things are going to work out. Just as I was excited to meet Scott, he was excited to meet me. And of course, he was nervous too.

As soon as he hung up the phone, he immediately grabbed his two-year-old son Marcus, put him in the car, and drove down to the mall to meet me. Soon, he had parked the car in the mall parking lot—it was just a short drive, as it turned out. He put his son on his shoulders and began walking quickly through the mall, heading to the payphones.

The mall wasn't very busy. As he looked around the area where the pay-phones were located, he realized nobody was waiting there.

How strange, he thought. *Where could Dixie be?*

He looked around again, totally confused by the absence of people. From inside the store, I watched him, wondering if this could be my son. I wasn't sure, so I waited. He walked past an older woman sitting on a bench near the phone bank. She was grey-haired, and she had a bag full of clothes sitting on the bench next to her. Her face had a worn-down look, much like you'd expect a stereotypical bag lady who is experiencing homelessness to appear. This woman was the only person in view who would have been old enough to be his mother.

This must be Dixie, he was thinking. *Should I hug her? Is it really her? What should I do?*

He walked by the woman again, studying her quietly, his son still on his shoulders. Feeling uncomfortable and unsure, he debated what to do. Suddenly, a wave of love and compassion rolled over him, and he found himself praying quietly to God.

"Okay, Lord," Scott said softly. "If that's my mother, then that's my mother. I don't care what she looks like. I don't care if she *is* a bag lady. I'm just going to love her."

I didn't know what he was doing at the time; I found out later. But as I watched him, I could see the look of compassion on his face. I realized that this young man was fully prepared to embrace the elderly woman on the bench, even if she did seem to be a bag lady, with all the issues that might involve. And if he was prepared to open his heart to her, then he was ready to open his heart to me.

Quickly, I exited the store and headed toward him. He had his back to me, and he was moving toward the bench to hug the elderly woman. Just before he could do so, I gave him a quick tap on his shoulder.

He turned around, and I saw a handsome young man who was dark-complected with curly hair just like his father Ernie's. He had a look of relief on his face. On his shoulders sat my grandson, a cute little boy that I fell instantly in love with. I smiled and said, "You must be Scott. I'm Dixie."

Later, Scott told me how much that moment meant to him. He was relieved to see me, looking "elegant and beautiful," as he put it. He and I didn't look like each other. With his dark hair and eyes, he clearly favored his father, Ernie, while I am fair-complected and have blue eyes.

"Your smile is amazing," he told me. We hugged each other, and then he invited me to follow him home. New Castle isn't that big, and before I knew it, I was parked in front of his lovely house and walking inside to meet his wife, Amy.

We all spent a wonderful time visiting with each other that week. We took long walks together, just talking and sharing our lives with each other. We found ourselves opening up to one another. Scott and I shared things with each other that we had never shared with anyone else. And we had much in common that made it easier for us to relate to one another.

For one thing, Scott and I had spent much of our childhoods feeling alone in a way. He was an only child, so he didn't have siblings to share his feelings and dreams with. I had a sister and a brother, but we weren't close, so I felt alone. Scott could understand what that was like, and I could understand what life had been like for him.

Moments like that just filled our talks. Both of us felt an immediate closeness, a connection that can only be explained by our bond as mother and son, something God had created that cannot be denied. I cannot quite describe the feeling, even now. We both were overwhelmed, overjoyed, and oh, so grateful!

All too soon, I had to return home. Looking out the window of the airplane, I couldn't help but be grateful that God had answered my prayers. I pulled out pen and paper, and I wrote this letter to Scott immediately, right there on the plane. I finished it later, as soon as I got home and had a chance to share all that had happened in Pennsylvania with Doug, Mark and Ray.

My Dearest Son,

I couldn't wait to write you, so I'm starting this letter on the airplane home. In between tears, I've sitting here looking out the window at God's Heaven and remembering this past week, every minute of every day from the time you said, "I don't know how to say this — this is the hardest thing I've ever had to do — I'm your son." Those three words and your voice are engraved in my heart forever.

I have never opened up to anyone as I have you, son. Our long walks and talks made me feel like there is a special bond between us now. Watching you these last few days, your strength, your complete faith in God, your love for everyone has given me the strength I needed to start my life anew. *Through your strength and faith, I have found the opening on the path back to God. With your love, faith and understanding, I have finally started that seed I've been wanting to plant but never had the courage or strength to do it before, I just know I can make it grow because I'm finally at peace with myself. I also know it will take time, but after seeing you and your complete faith and knowing I've been forgiven for my past, I know I can do it.*

I have truly been blessed with three wonderful sons. I'm so proud of you, Scott. You're a wonderful husband, father, and the youth of your school just glow with admiration for you.

I want to write your mother a note in the next few days, because I have a great deal of admiration for her. It took great strength, courage and love for her to do what she did. Her willingness to share your life with me is an act of true mother's love, and I'll be grateful to her for the rest of my life. Being able to be part of your life again and able to say I'm your mother is a prayer truly answered by God.

Your whole family and Amy's family made me feel so welcomed and seemed to welcome me as part of your family that I have just been overwhelmed and lost for words. Well, we're about to land so I'll continue this later.

Doug and Mark met me at the airport, and it took me about three hours to tell them all about you and my new family. Mark decided not to mess with you when he saw your picture. Haha! Everyone at work says you and I look alike and how handsome you are. The first question out of their mouths was is he married? Then I showed them pictures of your wonderful family.

Doug wants to know what kind of video you have, Beta or VHS. He wants to videotape everyone and send it to you.

I went to the doctor and got the stitches removed finally. The doctor said the tumor was benign, so now I can stop worrying.

The news on my father isn't as good. He had the vein blockage test done Tuesday and one side of his neck is 70% closed and the other is 60% closed. After the test, they think he had a mild heart attack so he had to stay in the hospital. I'm afraid he wouldn't make it if he went through with any surgery.

Be sure to let me know how your tournament comes out. I'll be thinking of you all weekend.

I've been reading the books you gave me when I ran across your baby pictures you gave me. I still don't know how you knew that was the one baby picture I wanted more than any. I want to write your age on the back, but I'm not sure how old you were.

I'm sending some pictures that you may keep if you want. I found the pictures taken of me at the airport two weeks after you were born when I was on my way to California.

I've been listening to your tape over and over and you're right, son, you should spread the gospel. You're so inspiring.

Well, I guess I better stop. You're probably getting tired of reading this. Give Amy and Marcus a hug for me. Remember, son, I love you more than words can express. God bless you all and keep you safe.

All my love,

Dixie

As I put the letter into an envelope and mailed it, I knew my life was never going to be the same again. This meeting I had with Scott wasn't just a moment in time. It would be the beginning of a wonderful relationship. I had missed the first twenty-seven years of his life, but I wasn't going to miss anymore.

In addition to sending a letter to Scott, I wrote to his mother, Marge. I wanted her to know how much I valued all she had done to bring us together. I want to share it here, both as a testimony to how wonderful a woman she was, and also as an encouragement to anyone who has adopted a child and is in Marge's shoes right now.

Dear Marge,

I wish I knew the words to express my admiration for you. I know it took great strength and courage to give my name and telephone number to your son. Your going to the trouble to search for all the information and giving it to Scott shows true and unselfish love for your son.

I don't want you to ever think I'm a threat to you for Scott's love or that I would ever interfere with his life and yours. I'm deeply thankful that you're willing to share him with me. I have been through so much mental torment these last 27 years not knowing if he was alive, well or happy. I was truly blessed by God when He chose you and your husband to raise my son. No one could have done a better job than the two of you did. Scott is truly a wonderful man and a son we both can be proud of. Thank you from the bottom of my heart for giving me the opportunity to know and love him after all these years of not knowing if he was even alive.

I hope that we can always be friends for I know if it hadn't been for your unselfish love, I would never have been able to have peace of mind.

If you ever get out to California, be sure to come and visit. I'm still so overwhelmed by your warm and loving family. Please say hello to everyone for me and thanks again for everything.

    Love,

    Dixie

Marge wrote me back and said, "I know how I would have felt if it had been me. And I also knew you would be the kind of person you are by the way Scott is warm and loving. Thank you again for giving Ed and me the opportunity to raise him. He was a joy and still is." She also told me that when she saw how happy Scott and I were to meet each other, she was even more glad she did what she did.

To this day, I'm still grateful and amazed at Marge's courage, strength, compassion and generosity of spirit. I believe God opened her heart toward sharing Scott with me. But I also know that she could have refused to help Scott reach out to me, especially since she didn't know what the outcome would be. She could have chosen a different path. But she didn't. Her love for Scott and her kindness toward me are something Scott and I will always treasure.

Two weeks after Scott met me, he had another miracle in his life because of what God was bringing about, with Marge's help. He got to meet his biological father, Ernie.

While we had visited, I had told Scott all about Ernie, who he was, and why we didn't get married. I had no idea where he went or what happened to him, so I couldn't tell Scott how to reach him. I thought it just might never work out that they could meet.

But Marge had other plans. Somehow, she managed to track Ernie down, just as she had done with me. And so, two weeks after Scott met me for the first time, he walked in the door of his home, dirty and sweaty from playing a ball game. And Marge was there.

"Go get cleaned up, and do it fast," she said. "Your dad is going to be here in ten minutes."

Shocked and excited, Scott hurried to get changed. And soon, Ernie was pulling up to the curb, in a red convertible with a white top. In the back seat was a basketball, football, and a set of golf clubs. The car was so similar to the red GTO Scott used to own, right down to the sports equipment in the back seat. *God, You are so amazing*, were the words that came to Scott's mind.

As soon as he saw his father, it was like looking in the mirror, he later told me. "It didn't take long to see who I took after," Scott said. They shared the same dark complexion and curly hair too.

They also shared their physical prowess. Scott's adopted father, Ed, loved sports but he was not athletic. When he and Scott would play catch, Ed frequently missed the ball. But Scott told me, "That didn't matter. Dad never missed one of my practices and attended every game in every sport I played. He was my biggest fan!"

So, Scott had always wondered if he'd inherited his abilities from his parents. And he had! Ernie was very athletic, and he loved football, basketball and baseball, just as Scott did. He also played golf and was a golf coach, teaching at a high school just forty-five minutes away from New Castle. Ernie eventually taught Scott and his youngest son,

Micah, to play golf, something they all three would share together. He also owned a beer distributorship and was very well known and well liked in his community.

"Ernie and I hit it off immediately because we had so much in common," Scott told me. "And because he was a golf coach, he inspired me to play golf too. I fell in love with it."

Golf had a significant impact on the course of Scott's life. Before this time, he hadn't considered pursuing golf at all, but because of Ernie's example and encouragement, Scott took up the sport too. And so did his son Micah. In fact, Micah quickly became the number one player on his team all throughout high school, which would never have happened if he and Scott had not met Ernie.

Scott and Micah became so enthusiastic about the sport that they found employment at a golf course, which allowed them to practice and play for free. He and Micah studied, practiced, and passed their PGA Player Ability Test, which opened up even more golf opportunities for them. Because of this, Scott is now manager of Castle Hills Golf Course, something he continues to do today—all as a result of meeting Ernie.

And because Ernie had other children, Scott gained a bigger family than he'd had growing up as an only child. He became close to Ernie's two daughters, especially the oldest daughter, Robin, whom he was able to lead to the Lord.

Later that year, I returned again to Pennsylvania to spend some time at Christmas with Scott and his family. And I was able to visit with Ernie as well. It was such a blessing to see him once again and remember the good times we'd had when we were teenagers.

Ernie shared more of his story with Scott and me. I'd been sneaking letters to him while I was in the Florence Crittendon unwed mothers home. He had wanted to come back and marry me, and then we would get Scott back. But he was in training in the Marine Corps, and he couldn't leave the base without going AWOL. By the time he was free to return, I'd already given Scott up for adoption, and I didn't have the heart to wrest him away from his new parents.

Even though we'd lost our son, Ernie still wanted to come back to marry me. He really had loved me as much as I loved him. But while he was still on the base, he got extremely ill and couldn't leave when he thought he'd be able to. By the time he'd recovered and was well enough to come for me, it was too late. I'd already gone to California. In a way, I'd vanished. He never could find me.

We finally reconnected through Scott—and through the efforts Marge made to bring us all together out of love for her son. That Christmas reunion was an amazing time of God's grace and mercy and restoration. I was just so happy to know that Ernie's life had gone well and that he'd had other children, and also that he could meet our son.

Scott was able to spend nearly twenty years in relationship with Ernie, enjoying each other's friendship, going on trips together, and sharing their love of golf and other sports. Ernie died at the age of 63, and Scott was able to speak at his funeral. It gave him and me both a sense of closure.

You see, it can be easy to second-guess the things we've done over the years. But God works out all things for our good when we trust

Him and allow Him to work in our lives as He wills. Scott says it like this:

"There are a lot of things in our lives that we don't have answers for. We have to do the best we can with what we do know, and every day press on toward the mark of our high calling in Christ. By doing that, we gain more and more knowledge and get more and more answers for all those questions."

And on top of that, we can always love one another, even if time and distance and circumstances have separated us. Scott wrote about it in a letter after meeting Ernie, and I think it's beautiful and powerful, so I want to share his words with you.

"There is a love where two people can enjoy the same things and be happy just to be with one another. A love that sees no faults, that has no pride. A love that is longsuffering and forbearing, that is always giving and is unconditional. It builds you up and never tears you down. A love that loves you for who and what you are, no matter who or what you are. This kind of love always prevails over evil and always makes bad situations into good ones. It's the love God has for us... I also know that it doesn't come overnight, but it's awesome and it's available to all who are willing to do what it takes to have it."

That is the love God has for us, and it's the love that has brought about our reunion as mother and son, in spite of everything that happened to separate us.

CHAPTER NINE

What's Lost Is Now Found

After meeting Scott and reconnecting with Ernie, I had to return to my normal life. This was so hard!

I returned to California, going back to my job at Lockheed Martin and being a mother to Mark and Ray and a wife to Doug. But there wasn't a day that went by that my thoughts weren't with Scott or focused on the past. There were times I just wanted to forget the rat race, return to Pennsylvania and be close to Scott.

It didn't help that my relationship with Doug was not going well at the time. We were growing apart. But I'll get to that in a moment.

After the typical bouncing around that we did as a military family over the years, Doug finally got orders that brought us back to San Diego, and that's where we remained until he retired. Over the years, he was often gone for six months out of the year, so the times we could be together felt special. We had a good life in many ways. But we experienced several bumps in the road too. I believe some of our struggles were tied to traumatic experiences that he went through while in the military.

Sadly, Doug was never the same after his time in Vietnam. During the war, he was chief of the sonar division, in charge of the big guns on his destroyer. It was a position with both prestige and a lot of pressure.

He was given orders to shoot any foreign boats out of the water if they came near the U.S. naval ship he served on. Well, one day a small Vietnamese boat started to head toward the ship. A Vietnamese woman was standing up in front of the boat, holding up her baby. But there were soldiers with guns hiding behind her. It was a common tactic of the Vietcong to use civilians this way. Doug had to give orders to shoot the boat out of the water.

Situations like that were hard on him. If he served in the military today, they might diagnose him with post-traumatic stress disorder. But back then, he was just expected to go on about his life. The pressure and pain he felt changed him. I tried to support him and be there for him as much as I could.

When he retired from the Navy, we moved away from San Diego and bought a home in Alta Loma, California. By then, our children were out of school, married or working. Doug and I both started working for Lockheed Martin. What I'd hoped would be a time of growing closer became just the opposite. We had trouble communicating and getting on the same page about things. Our relationship began to go downhill. Doug started seeing other women on the side.

It was heartbreaking, especially since I truly loved him. I begged him to go to counseling with me, so that we could talk things through. I was willing to do what needed to be done to make our relationship better. But he seemed totally uninterested in doing so. At times, he was even cruel about it, telling me he found me unattractive and that he didn't want to share a bed with me.

Soon, I was told by several coworkers that he was having an affair. And I even caught him with her one day. At the time, I was home from work because I was recovering from a surgical procedure. My recovery was painful, and I needed to get to the doctor to be checked out. So I called Doug at work.

"Would you come home and drive me to the doctor's office over your lunch break?" I asked.

"I'm too busy, Dixie. I'm at work!" he said.

So, I ended up driving myself to the doctor. On my way home, I pulled off the freeway onto the side streets, and there was Doug's car ahead of me. And there was his mistress, sitting beside him, laughing and having a good time. It was like dealing with Don all over again. I had tears in my eyes as I got home, devastated.

We had two dogs at the time, and Doug insisted that both dogs sleep with us in a full-size bed. It was uncomfortable, and I hated it. One day I gave him an ultimatum.

"Either those dogs sleep in their beds, or I'm going to sleep in the other bedroom," I said.

"I'll take the dogs," he answered.

"What is wrong with you, Doug? Why are you treating me like this?"

"You turn me off," was all he would say. I couldn't get him to explain himself any further.

On top of the tension in our marriage, I became worried about our finances and my job. The company I worked for was in the process of laying people off. *Would I be one of them?* I asked myself.

During these struggles, I couldn't help wondering what might have been if Ernie and I had gotten married. Would we have been happy? Would he have shown me the love I longed for? Would I have had the love, affection and happiness that I was still seeking and felt I'd been missing out on?

I dreamed of a different life, one in which I felt fully content and cared for. It was true that in many ways, Doug had been good to me. And we did have material things. But the love, affection, closeness and time together that I craved so much wasn't there. I wanted more, and I didn't know if it was possible to have more or if God wanted me to stay where I was and be content with what I had. I felt so confused, unable to stop thinking about Scott and Ernie, what might have been and what could still be.

And the worst part of it was that I couldn't understand what had happened between Doug and me or how to fix it.

Eventually, I considered getting a divorce. If I had to, I'd live with one of my sons until I could get back on my feet. So, I went to see my sons, Scott, Mark and Ray and their wives; it was the first time we were all together as a family. I told them I was going to leave Doug. They knew what I was going through and they supported my decision. As I was talking to them, I started to cry, and I took a walk alone. As I prayed over the situation, I felt in my heart that God was telling me to keep my oath to him and stay with Doug "until death do us part."

So, I didn't leave Doug after all.

Instead, Doug and I retired to the hills of South Dakota, where we built a home on twelve beautiful acres. At the time, Doug talked to me and said, "Dixie, things are going to be different from now on. I promise you. It will be better."

I thought I knew what he meant—that we were both retired now, and we had more time to be together. We would work on our marriage, and it would get better. So, I stayed with him. But his poor behavior and treatment of me continued. He remained distant and uncaring.

Still, I could see that he wasn't himself. He wasn't well. I quickly noticed how often he would cough and even choke. For fifty years, he had smoked up a storm. So as I watched him struggle for breath, I became concerned. I urged him to see a doctor. When he finally agreed to do so, he was diagnosed with cancer of the throat.

For eleven years, he fought sickness. He went through radiation and chemo treatments, and he even went in remission for five years. But during a checkup, they found lung cancer. He ended up having 154 radiation treatments, five different cancers, Crohn's disease, and shingles. He lost his voice, and had to eat by drinking fluids through a tube in his stomach.

I prayed to God. "If Doug isn't going to get well, Lord, please take him home and let him rest in peace."

Finally, after one final throat surgery, he passed away. It was a Friday afternoon. I thanked God for answering my prayer, for Doug was finally at peace and home in Heaven. We had forty-four years together, and my only wish is that we could have been happier together.

Yes, I could have left Doug when things got hard. But I chose to honor my marriage vows, even if he had not always done so. Seeing him through this time of sickness was very difficult, but I did it because I loved him, because we'd had many happy times together, and because I felt that God wanted me to stay with him. In the end, we were married for 45 years before Doug passed away.

And no matter what struggles we may have had in our years of marriage, Doug did something for me that I will always be grateful for. He supported me and encouraged me when the miracle I'd prayed for all those years—knowing Scott was ok—finally came to pass.

Right after Doug passed away, I went home to check on our dogs. It was late at night. Something was clearly wrong with my pomeranian, Jingles. She couldn't move. I lay on the floor with her all night and called the vet first thing the next morning. They picked her up and brought her to the animal hospital to examine her. That afternoon, I received a call.

"I'm so sorry," the vet said. "We had to put Jingles down because she was so sick and in so much pain. There was nothing else we could do for her."

I just felt my world was coming apart.

A week later, Doug's English springer spaniel, Rusty, lost control of his back legs. Whenever he moved, he would yelp in pain. I called the vet again. And Rusty also had to be put down. In one week, I lost everything.

There was nothing to stay in South Dakota for any longer. I sold the house, and three months later, I moved to Missouri to stay with my son, Ray, and his wife, Dayna, on their ranch. They were so good to me; they did so much for me, and I was grateful.

But I was so lonely too, because I spent so much time by myself. Ray and Dayna had jobs during the day, and in their spare time they also had to care for the ranch, which was quite large. I didn't know many people around town, so I would stay home most of the week, alone. I would spend my time tending the garden while they were at work.

One day, I prayed to God about it. "If I am to be alone for the remainder of my life, please help me to be satisfied with where I am," I told Him. "Let me just be content."

Not long after this prayer, I took a trip to Pennsylvania for my six-tieth high school reunion. It gave me a chance to visit with Scott and Amy, as well as see some old friends and relive some happy memories from my past.

It was a wonderful trip! I visited with all my girlfriends and sat next to my junior high boyfriend Bob Brush, who lost his wife to cancer six years earlier. We talked about that, and our lives and how much things had changed. But we also reminisced about our school days and had fun just laughing about old times.

The next day, the girls and I went to our high school football game. Bob came too, and again he sat beside me. It was as if we'd never been apart; the years just seemed to fade and we enjoyed each other's company as much as we did so many years earlier.

Bob asked if he could take me home after the game. He was so polite, such a gentleman, and it made me feel so appreciated and cared for. He wanted to show me New Wilmington and how it had changed in sixty years. Of course, I said yes. We went somewhere every day while I was in town, talking and laughing and enjoying our friendship. I didn't feel lonely at all during our time together.

But when I went back home to Missouri, the aching loneliness started up again. Bob called me every day from his home in Pennsylvania, and the moments we shared in conversation and companionship were the highlight of my days. He even invited me to spend time with him in Florida. Meanwhile, I still didn't feel like I quite fit into the town I was living in. And it made me realize it might be time for me to make a change of some kind.

So, I took a walk in the woods. Everything was quiet and peaceful, leaves crunching beneath my feet, trees towering above me, birds calling to one another. I breathed deeply, taking in the fresh air, and then I prayed to God, asking him once again for guidance.

"Lord, if I am to spend the rest of my days alone, please let me be content," I prayed. And then I left it in His hands to show me what to do next.

The next time Bob invited me to go to Florida and meet his son and daughter-in-law, I took him up on the offer. We had a wonderful time together, and being with him felt right. In my heart, I knew Bob was God's answer to my prayers about whether I was to remain alone or not. So, when Bob and I began to discuss marriage, I said yes.

A year later, we went to Florida and got married on the beach. Scott walked me down the aisle, Amy was my maid of honor, and my grandson Micah (their son) was an usher.

I wrote my own vows for the ceremony, but I feel God was helping me say what was in my heart. Here's what I said as Bob and I pledged ourselves to one another:

"We have come full circle in our lifetime—from first grade to standing here before God, our friends and family, declaring our love for each other. We have experienced the joys and sorrows of life through our many years on this earth. We have loved and married before and raised our families. Then in our twilight years, when we least expected it, God, fate and class reunions brought us together again with love and joy as fresh as our youth. You are my friend, my companion, and my lover. I hereby pledge myself to be your faithful wife with a love that will endure for all the rest of our days."

I know God brought Bob and I together again because we were both lonely and lost. And now, instead of being alone, we have each other, and a total of five children between us—my three sons, and his two sons, and their wives and children.

These days, I live near Scott and Amy. We get to spend so much time together, a miracle only God could have worked out. And through them, I have found a small church that feels like a family to me. My life is finally complete.

By bringing Scott and I together, God blessed all of us in so many wonderful ways. We gained so much!

I now have my whole family reunited, with more children and grandchildren and great-grandchildren to enjoy. I was able to meet Ernie again and share with him the things he did not know about my life and what had happened to me. We were able to let go of the grief of losing one another and giving up our son. And I even found myself in a wonderful relationship in my latter years with my first sweetheart—a miracle if there ever was one. My heart is so full because of all the good that God has brought about for me.

And Scott has been so greatly blessed too. He no longer has to wonder about who his parents were, or why he was given up for adoption. He's had the opportunity to know two sets of parents, all four of us loving him and being grateful to have him in our lives. He has known a second father after his first one passed away. He's discovered who he looks like and who he takes after. As an only child, he had wanted brothers and sisters—and now, he has them through my family, Ernie's family, and Bob's family.

We're all able to support one another and be there to encourage one another. When one of us is in need, our extended families can gather around us and lift us up. We can pray for one another. What a gift it is to have our entire family with us. We all need other people in our lives, and now through God, we have that.

And more than anything, we have God. We have His love. We have His salvation. We enjoy His peace and His guidance. What more could we need?

CHAPTER TEN

The True Purpose of Life

For years, I've told God and Scott that I wished I could tell my story. If I could change just one girl's mind so that she would decide on adoption instead of abortion, I'd feel like I have proved that God does answer our prayers, show us mercy, and lovingly lead us on the right path if we truly believe and ask Him.

My biggest hope and prayer is that a young mother, much like me, will read my story and be encouraged to follow her convictions and choose life instead of abortion. I don't want someone else going through what I went through—being made to feel by my family that I should be ashamed for choosing to have my child.

And I certainly don't want young women to be left wondering what would have happened if their children had not been aborted.

You see, abortion is a terrible thing. It is choosing to end life, rather than choosing to promote life and honor life as God intends for us to do. It closes down possibilities with an awful finality. There are so many babies who aren't being born, and their purposes and plans aren't being fulfilled. One of them could have been the next Billy Graham, or the next George Washington, and we'll never know it.

The loss we're suffering because these children are not being born and fulfilling their purpose is hard to calculate. But it is huge. And we are all losing out because of the children who *should* be here, making a difference in the world, but aren't here because their lives were ended before they had a chance to become the people God intended them to be.

Fortunately, abortion is not the only option we have. We can choose life instead, through keeping the child or through adoption. Choosing life is a great gift, both to ourselves and to everyone around us.

My story is living proof that adoption is a great opportunity for those, like me, who cannot care for their child. It is wonderful for those couples like Marge and Ed, who long for children but can't have children of their own. It is invaluable for children like Scott, who have a right to live, and through their lives can make such an impact on the world around them.

There is a verse of scripture in the Bible that says, "Choose life, so that you and your seed may live." By choosing life, we invite God into our circumstances. And as we trust Him, He can work things out for good.

I realize it's not always easy to picture the good that will happen when we are in the midst of our struggles. In our lives, we all face difficult decisions and tragedies. Choosing life is not always easy, but it has positive effects down the road if we will face the difficulties with courage and faith.

In the end, choosing life is so rewarding. It brings about even more life. It brings hope. It brings opportunities to make a difference for others in ways that rejecting life can't do.

As I look back now at my life and at Scott's life, I can see how God had His hand on both of us the entire time. Even with the heartbreak I endured, and how much it hurt at the time I chose life for my unborn son Scott, I can look back now and marvel at how much I have received in return.

I believe God watches over all of us, and He is always ready to work in our lives if we will open up our hearts and allow Him to do so. By praying and allowing Him to turn around my heartbreaking situation, He was able to do miracles for me and Marge and Ed and Scott.

Looking back now, I know that God has restored everything I had lost, and He has given me so much more on top of it. I know I am truly blessed. And I have faith that what He has done for me, He will do for other mothers who long for Him to bring about restoration in their lives.

I prayed for twenty-seven years to know my baby boy was OK. This is a long time to wait. But at the end of it all, my prayer was answered. God heard me all throughout those many years of waiting and praying and staying faithful to trust Him to give me my greatest desire, no matter how long it took.

During those years of waiting, I believe God was putting everything into place just as it needed to be, so that at the right time, everything would be lined up just perfectly, so that Scott and I would enjoy the fullness of restoration God had planned for us. If it had happened any other time, one or both of us might not have been ready for this miraculous reunion. But it happened just when it needed to happen— and God knew what He was doing.

That is the blessing of trusting Him and patiently allowing Him to work as He wills.

There's another reason to choose life too—and that is *love*.

God makes it clear throughout the Bible that He loves people. He loves us so much more than we can even imagine! Even those who are evil can enjoy giving their children good gifts. Well, God is a hundred thousand times more loving and giving than that. He knew us and loved us even before we were formed in our mother's womb.

In God's eyes, we all matter. Each life matters. *All life matters*—because He is the Father of us all. He loves each and every one of us.

His love has such a purpose and power behind it. You see, He intends for there to be a snowball effect—He pours out His love on us, and we pour it out on others. In that way, we bring His love, His compassion, His kindness to those in need. And the world can become a better place because of it.

We can see this purposefulness not just in the good times, but in the tragedies too. I may have lost Scott for a time, but I had two other beautiful boys, Mark and Ray, who might not have been born if I hadn't met their fathers. Ernie had three children—Robyn, Ted and Jennifer—who might not be here if he had not met his wife after he and I were separated by circumstances.

If Scott hadn't been born, he wouldn't have a lovely wife, children and grandchildren right now. He has lived his life with purpose and continues to make a difference in the lives of those he meets. His purposeful, giving nature would be missing from this world if he weren't here. But by choosing life, Scott has been able to do what he is meant to do on this earth, and it is a beautiful thing to witness.

Yes, Scott too has faced difficult times. Sadly, one of his children, his son Micah, had his life stolen through drug addiction. Micah was addicted to opiate pain pills for thirteen years, something he'd first been prescribed while recuperating from a knee injury he sustained while playing high school basketball.

Opiate drug addictions have risen to epidemic proportions, along with abortions, as both can destroy families and people's God-given purpose. Even though Micah's life was cut short and full of challenges, he too has had an impact on those around him—an impact for good. Through his life and even his loss, he inspired those who knew him in rehab to keep fighting the good fight of faith.

Scott now supports the ministry of Renewal Ranch, which is in the business of Restoring Broken Lives through Christ, located just outside of Conway, Arkansas, which Micah had been a part of. This powerful nonprofit organization exists to see broken lives restored. They offer classes that consist of teaching hope and purpose, coupled with life skills and training to men in need of restoration. They also perform hours of community service to help their city thrive.

Renewal Ranch started in 2011 with eight men attending. Now, they are celebrating ten years of success, having helped 350 men so far to make valuable changes. Multiple graduates have gone on to directly serve their communities in successful positions and organizations, as well as to be more stable husbands and fathers to their families. Many of them have gone on to college to receive an education. One graduate is now a police officer, while another is the dean of a college. They are having an impact in the areas where they live, work and serve. Their lives matter too, after all.

By helping Renewal Ranch with fundraisers and support, Scott and Amy are able to assist other men like Micah who are struggling with addiction and need help. These men, young and old, are valuable human beings who have a God-given purpose. Their lives matter, your life matters, all life matters!

If I had given in to the pressure to have an abortion, then Scott and Amy wouldn't be here to understand parents like them who need comfort and encouragement and guidance over children with addiction. They would not be here to make a difference in the lives of the men at Renewal Ranch. All of our lives intertwine for a divine purpose that we should treasure.

As the Bible says, "What was meant for evil, God has turned around for good." He can work out anything and bring good out of tragedy, as we trust Him to do it.

My story is proof positive that God deeply loves each one of us, and that His greatest desire is to redeem us from our mistakes, failures and heartbreaks.

His love is always, always there for you. His power to turn your life around, bring about restoration, and do miracles is always available— no matter what. It doesn't matter what circumstances you find yourself in. It doesn't matter if you've done all the wrong things or are looking for love in all the wrong places. Nothing is too big for Him to forgive, redeem, and heal.

Jesus is so much bigger than our failures. That's what I discovered when I turned to Him to help me. That's what Scott discovered in his life. And you can discover it too. It can begin in your life right now, with a simple decision to turn to Him and call on Him to become a part of your life. Right now. In the circumstances you're in right now. No matter what you've done.

If you have struggled in your life… if you have had an abortion, or faced addiction, or had other challenges that have left you feeling like a failure, I want you to know right now that God loves you. He can forgive you, and you can be free to live your life for Him from now on.

All you have to do is ask. Ask Him right now to forgive you, set you free from your mistakes, and bring about good in your life. Ask Him to take charge of your life. Do it in faith, expecting Him to do it. And just see what He does for you, now that you have prayed and asked Him to help you.

Scott and I are praying for you too. May you know how deeply you are loved, and how much hope there is in choosing life.

A Closing Prayer from Scott and Dixie

As we sit here side by side, considering the story of our lives that we have just shared with you, we can't help but marvel at the goodness of God. Through our lives and our experiences with how miraculously He brought us together, we've learned one thing without a doubt: God loves us.

He loves you as much as He loves us—and He loves us completely. He cares about every detail of our lives. He hears and remembers every single prayer we've ever made. And He is fully willing to do what seems impossible in our lives and give us our greatest desires and dreams, if only we will follow Him and allow Him to work in us, in His way, in His time. As we trust Him and wait patiently and with confidence, following His plan for us, He will bring about the blessings we have longed for—no matter how much time may pass between the prayer and the answer.

Our prayer for you is that you will come to know how deep, how high, how wide, and how miraculous and majestic God's love is for you, personally. We pray that the things you've longed for, and hoped for, and waited for will begin to show up in your life, fully blessing you in the way He has blessed us in bringing us together as mother and son.

Thank you for giving us the opportunity to share our story with you!

Dixie and Scott